er.
auth

'Lisa Greer provides a candid, behind-the-scenes account of the challenging and occasionally frustrating experience of new philanthropists. The combination of the post-pandemic landscape and the largest wealth transfer in the history of mankind presents an existential threat to the 1.5 million+ nonprofits in the U.S. This book provides practical, urgent guidance on how to cultivate meaningful, lasting relationships with this new generation of philanthropists to not only survive these twin threats but thrive.'
Bart Houlahan, co-founder of B Lab

'Lisa paints an intimate, enlightening, and refreshingly frank portrait of the misaligned incentives in the world of giving—and how we can fix it. It is destined to become a playbook and roadmap for a new generation of practical idealists.'
Kate Mulling, co-founder of Thrive Market and board member of the Garden School Foundation, and Zach Frechette, co-founder of _Good_ magazine and advisor to the Collaborative Fund

'In the wake of COVID, philanthropy needs a complete reboot. Fortunately, Lisa Greer thought the system was broken before and has a proposal ready. In this compelling mixture of personal story and forceful research, Lisa Greer explains the flattery and pampering that worked to raise funds in the twentieth century is anathema to engaged philanthropists of the twenty-first. A successful businesswoman and caring member of the community who suddenly became a major philanthropist, Lisa Greer forthrightly lays out the social and personal case for fundraising's new rules of transparency, engagement, and authenticity.'
Dan Friedman, Director of Communications at the Shalom Hartman Institute of North America, former Executive Editor of The Forward

'As America's nonprofit world faces starkly challenging changes, both in the demography of donors and social and economic uncertainty, Lisa Greer has provided a critically important book which can serve as an invaluable guide to nonprofits and also to their donors. At a time when profound changes will challenge the nonprofit world, Lisa's book offers donors and recipients a rich menu of constructive and practical suggestions to enrich and strengthen the relationships between the nonprofit and the donor.'
Mel Levine, former US Congressman, lawyer, President of the Los Angeles Board of Water and Power Commissioners, member of the Board of Directors of the Pacific Council on International Policy

'Writing a check is not enough … _Philanthropy Revolution_ is a candid, insightful, and practical assessment of the field, recognizing the value of the donor's perspective.'
Sonia and James Cummings, Nathan Cummings Foundation

'Rightly or wrongly, philanthropy has become one of the most significant pillars upon which our global order now uneasily rests. But—like so many of our institutions and systems—it's operating in an outdated way, with enormous implications for a dizzying number of global priorities. Lisa Greer approaches this issue with an equal measure of personal experience and forensic system-wide analysis. The result is a book that should be required reading for donors, fundraisers, and anyone serious about social change and how to fund it.'
John Lyndon, Executive Director of the Alliance for Middle East Peace

'Lisa Greer's excellent and timely book is a must-read for all philanthropists and those who are passionate about achieving real and effective change, the more so as we contemplate life after COVID-19.'
Neil Blair, The Blair Partnership, Chairman of Lumos and Pottermore, agent to J.K. Rowling

'A masterful, philosophical, and yet practical book that will get you thinking about philanthropy, fundraising, and the nonprofit world very differently. Lisa Greer boldly and constructively challenges so many taboos and failed collective wisdom in the field. A breath of fresh air, with ideas, sound wisdom, and remarkable insights that could save the world of philanthropy from its own self-inflicted wounds and direct all involved to new, broader horizons.'
Professor Abdullah Antepli, Chief Representative of Muslim Affairs at Duke University, Senior Fellow of the Shalom Hartman Institute

'The study and analysis of philanthropy has been steadily growing, shedding light on important subjects such as overheads, charity rankings, accountability, and impact. Notwithstanding the significance of these issues, they omit one crucial perspective—how donors *really* think. In *Philanthropy Revolution*, Lisa Greer bridges this glaring gap. The book is a straightforward, practical, and compelling guide that includes intuitive, yet all too often neglected, reminders to see donors not as wallets but rather as smart and committed partners that, given the right opportunity, will ensure a nonprofit achieves maximal impact. This book is a must-read for nonprofit leadership and staff, development professionals, and even donors.'
Dr. Shira Efron, Policy Fellow of the Israel Policy Forum, Visiting Fellow of the Institute for National Security Studies (INSS), and Special Advisor on Israel to the RAND Corporation

LISA GREER
& LARISSA KOSTOFF

PHILANTHROPY REVOLUTION

How to inspire donors, build relationships, and make a difference

HarperCollins*Publishers*

HarperCollins*Publishers*
1 London Bridge Street
London SE1 9GF

www.harpercollins.co.uk

First published by HarperCollins*Publishers* 2020

3 5 7 9 10 8 6 4 2

A catalogue record of this book is
available from the British Library

ISBN 978-0-00-838158-5

Printed and bound in Great Britain by
CPI Group (UK) Ltd, Croydon

'Transparency is the currency of trust.'

Digital marketing and marketing technology
leader Christopher S. Penn

'Pressure can break pipes or make diamonds.'

Retired National Basketball Association
champion Robert Horry

CONTENTS

NO CHOICE BUT TO CHANGE

When I started writing this book, I was driven by the conviction that the bottom would fall out of the world of nonprofits, something I saw happening in eight to twelve years. What I didn't envision was the crisis that would occur as we approached publication – a global catastrophe so severe that it amplified need in unprecedented ways, and also threatened the charities that would normally respond to this need.

The Coronavirus pandemic still rages as I write this. And while it rages, nonprofits are trying desperately to stay afloat. They're struggling to make a difference, strategize about an uncertain future, and adapt their fundraising efforts, event calendars, and finances to a new reality. This has happened before. Events such as 9/11 and the Great Recession have profoundly tested the charitable sector before now, raising questions about what's effective and also accelerating necessary change.

This book, with its practicable combination of tactics and strategy, couldn't have been better timed. For anyone involved with nonprofits, it charts a way forward – whether you share my concerns about a future sector crisis, or you're responding to a global emergency, such as COVID-19.

In many ways, the title says it all: *Philanthropy Revolution*. A global pandemic and the resulting economic crisis simply made the message that much more urgent. This is because the scale of what we're facing in 2020, as well as its long-term consequences, will force those of us in the 'helping' fields to find solutions immediately. We'll need to implement some of these solutions right away, adopting a triage approach that ensures our nonprofits survive in the short term and our beneficiaries are supported, too. Then we'll have to rethink the way we do business, which is the point of this book in the first place, in order to protect our charities for decades to come.

The good news is that a revolution in philanthropy needed to happen. That a crisis of this magnitude forced it to happen is devastating, but I urge you to treat the disruption as a move toward change. Our sector was already vulnerable. Its arcane methods were starting to fail, especially with next-gen donors. So, let's use this moment to shore ourselves up: to adapt, innovate, and ultimately transform our organizations for success and stability in the long term.

In March of 2020, some of America's foremost experts on fundraising gathered for a Giving USA board meeting. Unsurprisingly, COVID-19 had derailed the agenda, so these experts used their time to consider how the sector should respond. Their main advice? 'Don't stop talking to big donors because the world is being shaken. Past experience shows some donors never forgive the charities that don't reach out in times of need.'

Yes, I have to add … *but*. For, as this book will show, it's not just about talking; the important thing is how you go about it. If giving matters more than ever, then donors matter too. And as a donor, I'm about to teach you how to reach out and how to *keep* reaching out – whether the world is 'being shaken' or a new future for the sector is cast.

Let's create that future together.

INTRODUCTION

WELCOME TO THE 1%

'We're seated at the chairman's table,' I whispered to Josh, taking his arm as we entered the banquet hall.

This was our first major event at Hillcrest Country Club, a storied place whose members have included Jack Benny, George Burns, Groucho Marx and Sidney Poitier. Josh and I had joined a few weeks before, following a year-long vetting process – just in time, as it turned out, for the Jewish Federation's annual fundraising dinner.

We were new to the world of philanthropy. In July of 2010, RealD (the 3D projection technology company that Josh and his partner had built from scratch) had its initial public offering on the New York Stock Exchange. We'd gone from living paycheck to paycheck to the 1%, literally overnight.

I still couldn't quite get my head around the idea that I'd never have to worry about money again. It meant no more clipping coupons for Target or patching together loans to afford college for the kids, and I didn't know how to retire the somewhat prudent approach that had always been part of my mental wiring.

The one thing I'd taken to – quite naturally, in fact – was giving. Even before Josh and his partners rang the ceremonial bell at the New York Stock Exchange, I'd pledged $1M to my synagogue. Together with Josh, I'd also started the process of endowing a chair at a major hospital. And I'd made a smaller (but still significant) gift on the advice of friends, in this case to the Jewish Federation of Greater Los Angeles, a $50M umbrella organization for social service programs, community advocacy, and Jewish engagement.

Although we'd had little interaction with the Federation before then, we were confident that it did good work. Many in the community had suggested to us that a gift to the Federation was something of a prerequisite for being taken seriously in the world of Jewish philanthropy, and that's what appeared to have happened. That night at Hillcrest, we felt privileged to be recognized by the organization, having been seated as we were at the table of its top lay leader.

We sat through speeches and chatted with guests, and at about exactly the moment we were starting to relax and enjoy ourselves, we noticed a vinyl folio on the table in front of us. It was pretty innocuous, the sort of thing you'd get your check in at the deli. Someone had produced it, I surmised, while our attention was elsewhere

That someone was the chairman, as it turned out. He must have seen us register that the folio was in front of us, because he immediately stood and made his way to my side.

I opened the folio to see what it contained: a ledger-like printout. Standing over me now, the chairman leaned in. 'This is last year's gift,' he said, pointing to a number on the printout. 'Of course, your gift this year will reflect a significant increase.'

He handed me a pen.

I remember catching Josh's eye above our wineglasses. We'd later discuss the fact that we sensed people watching us. Those around us were chatting, milling about, eating dessert or enjoying a coffee – but they were definitely watching. As I've explained, I'd made a significant donation to the Federation only a few months before. Now I had to increase it? We hadn't been told that the gift was annual and nor had anyone from the organization sought us out to identify the extent to which we were aligned with its values and mission.

We were so embarrassed. The club has a two-year probation period (ensuring compliance with its charitable donation policy) that neither of us wanted to breach, so we were also at a loss as to what to do. We asked the chairman if we could enter the same amount as we'd donated previously and left it at that.

But, in the car on the way home, we wondered aloud whether all the other donors out there were accustomed to being strong-armed in this manner, in public.

Was this philanthropy?

Of all the freedoms I anticipated having when our lives were so dramatically altered, the one that excited me the most was the freedom to give. Specifically, to give of our money. Josh and I had envisioned ourselves as active givers who would also be involved with the organizations we funded. We had hopes of addressing Crohn's disease (which Josh has lived with for decades) and child welfare, as well as advocating for democracy in Israel, among other progressive causes.

Today, Josh and I are the proud supporters of dozens of nonprofits, not only as givers, but also as volunteers and leaders. We both sit on boards and enjoy close relationships with executives and staff across the sector. In the last decade, we've also hosted nearly 200 charity events in the home we chose specifically for this purpose. In fact, our giving portfolio is such that I left my career as a businesswoman – in part so that I could give the portfolio the full attention it deserved.

So why this book?

All too often, my interactions with nonprofits have left me feeling that the only thing I've got is my money, and that some fundraisers have been taught from the get-go to make their single priority *acquiring* this money. My sense (not always, but often) is that I'm there to be 'worked' and coddled, manipulated into loosening my purse strings. And this has meant that everything I value – the qualities of honesty, transparency, and connection that have always governed my personal relationships, as well my relationships in business – is left at the door.

If this experience were unique to me, I'd probably just take that beautiful model I envisioned, when I sketched out our lives as givers, and put it in a box somewhere. But as you'll learn in these pages, I'm not alone in the experience. And philanthropy is paying the price.

A Deal with God

Even before the IPO, Josh and I decided that, if everything unfolded as it appeared to be unfolding, we'd each make a major gift to a cause that mattered to us personally.

I'd chosen the synagogue, the Reform congregation where our twins (who were four years old when our lives changed) attended preschool and where I was a vice-president on the board.

The Senior Rabbi had been a source of wisdom and calm for me during the stressful months before the IPO – and believe me, 'stressful' is putting it mildly.

The cocktail-party version of the RealD trajectory goes something like this: years ago, Josh became acquainted with film director James Cameron. This was by way of Josh's early work in digital-entertainment development, production, and marketing. But, in 1996, Josh and James began working on something different – something driven by the possibility that Josh could create the technology for clean and immersive 3D-viewing.

Josh is a self-trained inventor. By almost any measure, he is also a technological genius. Working at first in our garage, he set about creating a brand-new system of screens, projectors, and 3D glasses. Over the next decade, investors got on board and Josh's technology began hitting theaters in 2005. In 2009, James Cameron's blockbuster film *Avatar*, which was produced with RealD technology, showed on 4,000 screens in fifty countries, becoming the highest-grossing movie of all time.

Josh's technology not only revolutionized 3D, it remains the industry standard today. It would eventually catapult RealD into the global marketplace, leading to its IPO in July of 2010. At that time, the company was valued at $200M. Shortly afterwards, its valuation peaked at $1B.

But getting there – well, it took an awful lot out of Josh, and also out of me.

We married in 2004, and in 2006 had our twins, Jack and Emily. I had kids from previous marriages: Sasha and Darrow were teenagers when I married Josh, and Halley was ten years old. For his part, Josh wasn't a stranger to success; quite the opposite. He'd co-founded and sold Digital Planet, one of the first companies ever to build entertainment industry websites. But he'd put his assets back into RealD and didn't earn a salary from the company for many years. I'd left my job as a studio executive before we married to run my own media, entertainment, and technology consulting business, and I supported the family until Josh (following an infusion of investments into RealD just before the IPO) was able to draw an income.

At that point, we were doing fine. We'd purchased a small house and we obviously paid our bills, but we also had to go deeply into debt to cover the costs of the lawyers who would protect our interests and support us during the IPO. Which, I might add, came with no guarantees. We had no idea if we were about to be able to retire in luxury or spend the rest of our lives in monstrous debt.

Josh was also traveling non-stop in the weeks before the IPO (not good, given his Crohn's disease) and I was working, not to mention taking care of the kids, worrying about Josh and our family's future, and basically falling apart. So, I did what you do. I made a deal with God.

If we came out okay, I'd do something major for my synagogue.

One of the first calls I made after the successful roadshow (which is the step just before an official IPO) was to the Senior Rabbi at my temple. I told her that we'd be donating $1M to the synagogue's capital campaign. Needless to say, she was thrilled.

I was, too, until the moment she started grilling me.

The rabbi didn't question the fact that an IPO was imminent. She didn't have to – I'd already given her the option to buy some RealD friends-and-family shares, which is common practice in these scenarios. What she questioned instead was the gift, along with my ability (perhaps even my authority) to make a gift of this magnitude happen.

Within minutes of our hanging up, the rabbi called me back. She wanted to talk to Josh this time, because she needed to make sure, she told me, that he approved of this donation – and that I wasn't living in a 'fantasyland' or just being impulsive. It seemed to me as if my friend and supporter (frankly, my feminist role model) was calling to confirm *with my husband* that a financial decision I'd made was credible.

I might have seen this as telling – an early indication that, where large donations are involved, people will often behave in unexpected ways. I learned later that, with this simple call to the rabbi, autonomous 'me' had thrown off the system, or at least the system governing major donations. There had been no early qualifying discussion with a development director, no strategy meeting, no lunch with fundraisers and no 'ask' for money.

Still, we were very proud a few months later to dedicate The Greer Social Hall at Temple Emanuel in Beverly Hills. All the fuss of the occasion made me think of my grandmother, who used to point out my grandfather's plaque at the synagogue we visited on High Holidays. And it certainly would have meant a lot to my dad, who died when I was in my twenties.

As for us, it was a little surreal to see our family name on a wall. But it also felt good.

Lisa and Josh Who?

With giving now occupying such an important part of our lives, Josh and I decided that I should sell the egg-donor agency that I'd founded a few years earlier in order to help people who were struggling with fertility issues. Anyway, I was ready. Our lives had suddenly become a lot more complicated, and I wanted to dedicate myself full-time to managing our giving portfolio as well as some of our real-estate investments. In the intervening months, we'd put much of the RealD money into investments so that Josh and I wouldn't have to work another day in our lives if we so chose – which is laughable in retrospect, since neither of us can sit still for longer than five minutes. We also established trust funds for the kids and, on the advice of friends, set up a Donor Advised Fund at the Jewish Community Foundation.

We were ready to work on Josh's big gift.

Josh, who grew up in Toronto, was diagnosed with Crohn's disease as a teenager. He actually taught himself computer programming in high school in order to keep himself busy during the many months he was ill, either stuck at home or in the hospital. He has endured dozens of surgeries and years of pain, and has nurtured a vision, in the process, of building an institute dedicated to Crohn's research. We reached out to Cedars-Sinai Medical Center (a world-class hospital not far from where we live, and where Josh and our family have been treated for years) and what transpired offered us another clue that we had entered a whole new world.

A friend had opened the door for us by introducing us to the president of the board. Still, when Josh made it known that he wanted to make a major donation for Crohn's research, we were transferred to a junior development officer. We called several times over the next couple of months, but nobody took us seriously. A full *six* months after we first made contact, Cedars accepted our money.

A realistic interval for a large institution? Maybe. But with new donors like ourselves, who aren't accustomed to the delay (and who might not persevere through the silence), it's a risky way to do business.

What if we had walked?

I did realize later that, to these charities, we were pretty alien. We represented totally unknown entities. We hadn't progressed through any of the conventional channels of donor cultivation (such as the lunches and pitches and follow-up) and nor were we the product of prospect research. We didn't also throw numbers around or make demands, and they had no idea how to handle us.

Cedars has one of the most well-conceived and sensitively run development plans I've ever seen. That's what I realize now. The organization has even integrated its early experience with us into its development training, reframing what happened into a teaching moment for fundraisers. And without question, the day we dedicated the Joshua L. and Lisa Z. Greer Chair in Inflammatory Bowel Disease Genetics at Cedars in late 2011 was one for the books.

Even now, Josh and I feel overwhelmed by the idea that we might actually have an impact on a disease that has so profoundly affected his life. Dr. Dermot McGovern, a world expert in the field, assumed the role of Chair, and our donation has allowed him to take risks, explore different approaches, and leverage the initial seed money into additional grants and funding.

Also, the lab's work has been groundbreaking. It has generated practicable insights into specific genetic variations of Crohn's disease, resulting in certain customized therapies already entering clinical trial. Happily, we've also developed a friendship with Dermot and his wife, and Josh and I both serve on Cedars' Board of Governors.

But the lesson remains. Until you've got a name and a reputation as a donor, you may well find it hard to give your money away. And for a sector that's desperate to attract support, especially *new* support, so that its worthy nonprofits succeed, that's a problem.

Off Script! Off Script!

These early experiences gave us insight into the practices and politics of the sector, but it wasn't until I started taking meetings on a regular basis that I realized just how out of sync our philanthropic systems were with what I'd always known to be true about human beings.

It took about a year for our names to get out there. This heralded an onslaught of emails and calls, but I noted with interest the fact that, although I let it be known to fundraisers that *I* handle our family finances, everyone wanted to meet us 'together.'

I found some solicitations easy to decline. If a charity had nothing to do with my values or interests, I didn't bother. For the most part, though, I was dying to learn about the wonderful work of the organizations that were contacting me, and I very happily took the meetings – solo, more often than not – to the extent of scheduling several a week. In many ways, it was an education, an immersive 'master class' in charitable giving.

The only problem was that many of these meetings, perhaps even most, were disappointing.

I'll give you an example. A good friend of mine supports an organization dedicated to promoting tolerance and defending civil rights. This friend asked me to meet with the regional and development directors of her organization because these directors claimed to want to honor me at an event recognizing women's accomplishments.

I'd had nothing whatsoever to do with the organization prior to this news of my honor, and wasn't even sure that its mission and activities aligned with my interests. I also had yet to learn that this sort of 'honoring' almost always involves a donation, a sort of quid pro quo that has you 'give' for the 'honor' of the honor. We'll discuss this in detail in Chapter Eight.

Suffice it to say for now that I accepted the invitation to lunch, because it had come by way of a friend. My own parents had once held the organization doing the honoring in high esteem, and anyway, what did I have to lose?

We met at a café I'd recommended in Beverly Hills, and, only moments after the development directors had made their introductions, the fawning started. I looked great, the directors told me. My simple black purse was fantastic. Oh, and they'd heard so *very* much about me.

It was flattery of a sort that I'd never experienced, and I had to wonder what these women truly thought about rich ladies like me and our egos. We made small talk after that, and they continued to crow about everything they'd 'heard.' More praise here for me and my family. It became clear, however, that they really knew nothing about us. They certainly didn't know what my charitable interests were or what sorts of things typically motivated me to give.

One thing *I* know about myself is that I'm good at small talk. It's a skill I picked up in business. At Universal Studios, I served on the first team of executives responsible for establishing the organization's web presence. I moved to NBC after that, and later established a media, marketing, and technology consulting firm. So, I understand the formula: small talk and then substance. The point of the small talk is to get to know the client (or in this case, the donor) in a deeper way. Why? Well, you want to build a rapport on the one hand, and you also want to find the connection between the client's interests and your own. That's how you know how to 'ask' them to buy – or even support – whatever it is that you've got on offer.

In retrospect, the sad truth of that lunch meeting is that nothing those development directors said, and not one of the handful of questions they asked, was ever going to yield any insight – at least not regarding my giving. I came away convinced that all they knew, and definitely the only thing they cared about, was that I had money. My being a good match with what they were 'selling' was beside the point.

I did ask them some specific questions about the work of their organization, questions that had cropped up for me during my review of their website prior to the meeting. Doing research before a meeting is essential, no matter your business, but my line of enquiry appeared to surprise these professionals. Rather than answer my questions, one or the other would launch into a prepared pitch about why I should offer support.

'Is the anti-bullying program you mentioned being implemented at the local school?'

They didn't know. Back to the pitch.

'Does the organization collaborate with nonprofits doing similar work?'

They couldn't say. More of the pitch.

They might have offered to get me some answers. Instead, they tried to shoehorn their 'script' into the hole that had been left by my questions. To their credit, they did eventually offer to follow up with the information I'd requested, but not without also asking me to commit *then and there* to being honored. Which, as per the quid pro quo I described earlier, also meant a commitment to give.

Needless to say, I ultimately declined.

An Old-School Approach That's Pervasive

I sat through dozens and dozens of meetings just like this one in my first years of giving, *long* meetings characterized by the same old formulaic chumminess, the prepared scripts, and only nominal respect for my input. I began to dread the idea of 'lunch' – these meetings typically occurred over lunch – because 'lunch' meant that I'd be forfeiting my afternoon for another phony interaction with fundraisers. I wanted to spend time with my kids and devote attention to my investment and giving portfolios. I also hated the disappointment. Yet another bad meeting, I'd think, for an otherwise wonderful cause.

Since I consider my giving a direct expression of my values, it's always been imperative that I give thoughtfully, with attention to how organizations are run. I'm also an unrepentant 'fixer'. If someone has a problem, I'll twist myself in knots just to make things right. In the case of the fundraisers who wanted to 'honor' me (as well as with the Hillcrest dinner, the temple, and Cedars), I was eager to help. And not just by way of my wealth.

A lot of this has been personal, but I've got a business case to make with this book, which I'll start to lay out in subsequent chapters. In the meantime, I'm well aware of the challenges that fundraisers face on a daily basis. For one, rich people (that demographic on which the sector depends) can be notoriously difficult. Josh and I dealt with this stigma when we first became wealthy, and some friends of ours grew distant because they were certain we would change.

I get it. But I've also encountered so many people of means who are incredibly empathetic, generous with their time and money, and brimming with experience and skill. These are the givers the sector needs, just as it needs all those people with lesser means who have yet to find their way to philanthropy.

The problem is, if it's too risky to treat donors like people, if the humanity in this exercise has been depleted by revenue targets, or exhausted by the demands of the difficult rich, where does that leave us? Fundraisers have told me time and again that a single, unwitting slight to a donor can jeopardize years of relationship-building, not to mention that donor's support. Hence all the scripted, superficial, spiritless interactions that are designed to leave no room for error.

Philanthropy is in trouble, as we'll discuss in the next chapter. And while I agree that there's no room for error, what that means for me is the 'revolution' of the book's title – a rethink and a redo of our old-school ways and approaches.

I promise to help you through it. I used to wonder if what I was experiencing in the sector would change once I wasn't so 'new.' Maybe, if I met with enough fundraisers and eventually earned their respect, I'd feel better about the system. But what I've described in this introduction continues. And the 'new money' I represent? It's given me a lens that is also new. And valuable. It isn't just about the business experience (although I bring that to bear in these pages), it's about being ready and willing to question what the 'old money' takes for granted.

When you're a tourist in a foreign country, you see things that the regulars have long stopped noticing. New York pedestrians don't believe in red lights. Angelenos wave and nod their thanks when they encounter considerate drivers. The French sit adjacent at sidewalk cafés.

I could go on. The point is, you take notice. You do the little wave and slide your chair over. You adapt.

Or else you don't. In my case, you write a book.

I hope you enjoy it.

ONE

PHILANTHROPY IS IN TROUBLE

What Those Hundreds of Billions Are Hiding

When we first hired our business manager, not long after the IPO, I asked her how the other clients on her roster went about their charitable giving. These were the Hollywood-types and CEOs known by some segments of the financial services industry as 'High Net Worth Individuals' or HNWIs.

'Lisa,' she said, looking surprised that I had to ask, 'most of my clients just don't give.'

My experiences in the years since have confirmed this. I've learned that many people with wealth hold on to it. They consider giving but delay, or else park all their money in a Donor Advised Fund. I worry that, just like me, they've been put off once too often by the lack of humanity in fundraising, its outmoded approaches to the ask for money, or its pandering style of donor engagement.

In the next decade, many of our older donors, all those whose generosity has sustained our charities for years, will begin to pass away. And when this happens, if the sector doubles down by continuing to solicit the 'young' using tactics designed for the 'old,' our newest donors will walk. Ideally, these new donors will start philanthropies of their own. This is a trend that we're already seeing with organizations such as Swipe Out Hunger, which we'll discuss in Chapter Five. But, even if the trend continues, where will it leave all those big nonprofits that have helped to define us – not to mention feed our poor, build our concert halls, care for our sick, and fund our research?

Don't Be Fooled by $427 Billion

On the surface, fundraising looks like it's doing just fine.

The USA is home to an estimated 1.6 million nonprofit organizations. According to the latest Giving USA report, Americans are giving record amounts, with charitable donations jumping 5% from 2016 to 2017. As a whole, we gave $427.7 billion to charitable causes in 2018, with about 70% of that amount coming from individual donors, and the rest from foundations, corporations, and bequests. Over the past forty years, giving has held steady at about 2% of GDP, taking dips in recession years, and then recovering.

This can and should be a point of pride. As government continues to slash funding for social services, the arts, and scientific research, philanthropy has stepped into the breach. But these numbers hold a hidden truth. While the dollar amounts are up, household giving is down. Data from the Lilly

Family School of Philanthropy at Indiana University, the world's first and foremost school dedicated to the study and teaching of philanthropy, shows this to be the case across all income brackets, ages, and levels of education. In 2001, for example, 65% of households gave to charity, and that rate has been dropping. Already, in 2015, it had dropped to 55%. This downward trend continues, with the steepest decline noted in more recent years among donors aged fifty-one to sixty, the very people that, arguably, should be ramping up their giving (not only because they're part of the demographic of older Americans, which according to *Business Insider*, holds 80% of wealth, but also because most of them are earning still, often at the highest rate of their careers).

That many in the population aren't earning enough, or are otherwise struggling to make ends meet, is clearly a major factor – income inequality and wealth inequity are among the defining challenges of our time. But people aren't giving for lots of reasons.

How we feel about religion is one of these reasons. Giving to religious institutions accounts for more than 30% of all giving, and givers who call themselves religious tend to be among the most generous to all institutions, religious or otherwise. But according to a report from the nonpartisan Pew Research Center, religious affiliation is way down in America. And with it, religious giving. In fact, the number of Americans giving to religious causes has declined by about 50% since 1990.

Also upsetting the balance, so far as giving goes, are the young. Our younger generations give and relate to causes differently. They might install solar panels, for example, instead of giving to the Sierra Club. Or they'll give directly by way of online crowdfunding platforms. As we'll discuss in later chapters, they definitely prefer start-ups to our charitable giants and they also tend to be eager to experiment, so their loyalties shift more frequently than we're accustomed to seeing in the givers of old.

Interestingly, though, these generations hold sway. We're now starting to see that their ways are contagious, attracting new 'giving converts' from Generation X and even (I'll attest to this) among Boomers. The thing is, these generations aren't very keen on established models. Yes, they're beginning to give. And they're definitely engaging in a manner that's unique enough to inspire donors like me to take notice. But Millennials and Gen Y tend to give to the smaller and scrappier nonprofits. Or, they'll start their *own* nonprofits, a few of which we'll explore in later chapters. In either case, our traditional charities aren't seeing a lot of their charitable dollars.

An Unsettling Reliance on the Few

The truth about the increase in dollar amounts going to charities is that fewer people are giving more. This might continue to sustain some organizations, but it's also precarious, as it puts the responsibility for philanthropy into the hands (and subject to the whims) of the mega-rich.

As per the latest US Trust Study of High-Net Worth Philanthropy, 90% of households with incomes of more than

$200K or assets of more than $1M (excluding primary homes) donated an average of more than $29K, up 15% from 2015. US households gave more than 1,800 gifts of $1M or more in 2015, worth over $19B – a big jump from previous years.

Philanthropists such as J. K. Rowling (who fell out of the billionaires' club because she gave so substantially) and Warren Buffett (who encourages the mega-rich to divest of their wealth) might have us believing that system is sound. But it's deceptive, since the richest among us are really only giving a tiny percentage of their total net worth.

As *The Givers* author David Callahan concedes, 'Yes, affluent Americans have been giving more. But they've also been earning more, and it's far from clear that their giving has kept up with their new wealth accumulation. The top 1% has assets of $30 trillion, about a third of all household wealth. But these Americans gave away less than a half of 1% of their total wealth in 2016.'

THE UK ISN'T FARING MUCH BETTER

A Barclays Private Bank report published just last year has found that there are too few major donors outside the US, and the situation is having a significant impact on UK charitable funding.

'Barriers to Giving: Research into the evolving world of philanthropy' reports that as many as 47% of multimillionaires outside America donate less than 1% of their annual income to nonprofit causes.

Commissioned in partnership with The Beacon Collaborative and the Institute of Fundraising, the whitepaper also reports that philanthropic donations amount to just 0.5% of the GDP in the UK, compared with 2.1% in the US.

'Barriers to Giving' mentions an 'us and them' mentality between the wealthy and charities, the product of little understanding and poor communication. And, significantly, charities' current methods of 'engaging' with high net worth individuals (or HNWIs) are identified as considerable barriers to major giving.

Additionally, the findings tell us that 75% of HNWIs believe philanthropy is a responsibility of those wealthier than themselves, and 42% believe that making extra donations wouldn't be enough to have a significant impact.

It's important to consider, too, that the Warren Buffetts of the world are skewing our numbers. Those who give in the billions make up for all the millionaires who only ever part with a couple of thousand dollars. That average of $29K a year in charitable dollars might be acceptable for people at the lower end of what constitutes high-net worth, but the minute you're looking at your boat and your multiple homes and all the investments you don't want to part with – it just doesn't seem right.

My overwhelming sense is that many who have the privilege of occupying this space, people who frankly look a little like me: they're not giving what they should. I could go on for days about the reasons why (and I will, in subsequent chapters) and I've already made the point in these pages that purposeful giving takes time. Some people hire philanthropic advisors when they don't have the time, or they set up foundations that others can run – and good for them for doing so. It's the ones who plan to give *eventually*, or who decide to let their kids sort it out when they inherit; these are the folks we need to get on board.

We'll look in detail at what motivates donors in Chapter Two. It's enough to say for now that those who lack motivation are missing out. Despite my issues with the sector, seeing our money help others has been one of the greatest joys of my life. So very often, I get to be living proof of the studies (ubiquitous these days) that tout the physical and psychological benefits of giving for the giver.

Unfortunately, I've also become acquainted with some ugly truths. For one, I'm convinced that people aren't giving as much because the process of giving is fundamentally flawed, unproductive, and often downright unpleasant. It's probably been flawed forever. But our donors have changed where the system hasn't, and the disconnect is apparent – it's even expressed by donors when they're surveyed. So, the question is this: if today's fundraising tactics actually preclude connection, instead of fostering it, will people continue to give?

It's Not Just Me

I'm about a decade in, philanthropically speaking, and my sense of wonder has become one of alarm. But, again, I'm an unrepentant fixer, and when I started questioning accepted practices in fundraising, I also started talking to friends and colleagues. I asked the nonprofit professionals I now knew, as well as other donors, to be candid about their experiences.

I needed to first understand if I was an outlier. Was I over-eager? Too intent on connection? Too focused on business? Too interested in truth?

No, as it turns out. I wasn't. I've spoken since to dozens and dozens of philanthropists and development professionals, and nearly all of them corroborate my experiences.

Part of the issue is what I was getting at earlier. The sector is profiling donors (and interacting with them, too) based on criteria that are no longer relevant. Or at least not relevant in the main. When we had our IPO, for example, stockbrokers and real-estate agents found us and approached us immediately. It took most charitable organizations a good year to do the same – and we'd already made significant gifts!

I've heard similar stories from others, those who don't fit the mold of your typical giver. I've talked to Asian American philanthropists who constantly get overlooked, despite the fact that they give in the arena of hundreds of thousands of charitable dollars, if not more. In my home state of California, Chinese Americans gave more than $50 million in major gifts in 2017 to UC Berkeley, UC San Francisco, UCLA and UC Irvine. In fact, donations from Chinese Americans accounted for 1.2% of all major US philanthropic gifts between 2008 and 2014 – a percentage that was roughly proportional at the time to their population of about 4 million.

Often discounted, too, are women philanthropists and donors of color, with the latter group so lacking in recognition that a movement was initiated almost a decade ago to designate August as Black Philanthropy Month. The idea was to draw attention to *centuries* of generosity among people of color – a donor population that many nonprofits continue to ignore.

Young people don't fare much better. My older kids have joined a funding network called Resource Generation (see pages 68–9), where young people with wealth take the time to really consider where they give, and how their giving can be part of a more equitable system. I've spoken to my kids' peers, however, about how often thoughtful Millennials like themselves are relegated to 'junior seats' on boards. They're courted and coddled (often patronizingly so) and their volunteerism is welcome, as is their money. But do they get a voice? Not often enough.

When I took on our giving portfolio, I was shocked at the number of professionals who insisted that Josh (surely the holder of our purse strings, in their arcane world) come along on our lunches. Some of them even tried to go *around* me to get to him. Many of my girlfriends have comparable stories, and they've shared their feelings of frustration about sexism in the sector in general. It's about all those ladies' luncheons in the middle of the workday, the chaperoning husbands, and the old-school fluff – just thinking about it makes my skin crawl.

As for the phony relationships, I figured out quickly (though not quickly enough) that nearly any time I received an invite from a fundraiser – for breakfast, lunch, a cocktail or a playdate with kids – I would get pitched. It exhausted me: trying to figure out which of these dates were social and which were business. Of course, fundraising is built on relationships. A power imbalance exists within these relationships (we'll look at this in Chapter Three) and that makes them challenging. But why are we pretending we're 'besties'? Why can't we just be straightforward?

FUNDRAISERS AREN'T HAPPY EITHER

On average, a development director will spend just eighteen months at any given organization. Some studies put that tenure at sixteen months and suggest that the vacated positions are hard to fill. There are many reasons for this. The high demand for qualified talent, for example, means that good people get headhunted. And a major issue is under-resourcing: these professionals often get little support from their organizations and nothing in the way of career development, all while managing serious expectations related to revenue, and a whole lot of pressure to connect personally with donors.

A recent survey conducted for the *Chronicle of Philanthropy* and the Association of Fundraising Professionals revealed that 51% of fundraisers said they'll leave their current nonprofit with the next two years, while 30% said they'll leave fundraising altogether. A full 55% of them felt underappreciated often and (maybe worst of all) 21% agreed that the negatives outweighed the positives when it came to their jobs in fundraising.

Development directors of organizations large and small spoke to me with great candor about the pressure they feel to develop close 'relationships' with donors. They told me that sometimes (perhaps even often) the connection is real. When it isn't real, however, or when it hasn't had time to show itself yet, these professionals have to feign friendship – even if they share little in common with the donor, or worse, the donor treats them like crap.

You start to see (or I did, anyway) why fundraisers might put their guard up, not realizing that being clear and professional – as opposed to *un*clear or artificially personal – is so much easier on donors. It lets donors know where we stand.

My friend Peter, who comes from a philanthropic family and has been in the game for years, told me he almost always feels he's got a target on his back. He's used to it and continues to give, but he's also become really cynical. He wonders why he stays with it.

Miriam, a passionate businesswoman and major donor, described how she'd invested in a mentorship project whose focus was young women in business. The organization running the project shut Miriam out of any discussions about the project after she'd made her donation. And it broke her heart, she said, to realize that the fundraisers' initial interest in her perspective was simply their way of humoring her. They didn't want her ideas, or even her experience; they only wanted her money.

Alissa, who volunteers each week with at-risk youth, told me she prefers being a 'volunteer' to a 'donor.' She gets treated better, she says – but why can't she be both? (Alissa's 'favorite' donor moments, incidentally, involve her being asked to sit on phony 'strategic' committees, just so that she'll give more money.)

Then, too, donors who get meaningfully involved with their volunteerism can sometimes pose a threat – whether real or perceived – to the organizations they serve. My friend Greg 'caught' the organization he supported hiding serious financial problems from its board (a board on which he sat) because nobody wanted the fallout from donors. In this case, the put-on-a-happy-face-for-donors approach almost led to an organization's collapse.

SECTOR STEREOTYPES AND LADIES
WHO LUNCH

For most donors and fundraisers, the tired old ways of doing things are taking a significant toll. But there *are* donors out there who enjoy the evening-gown dinners and the 'wink-wink' lunches (where a pair of fundraisers seek to flatter a donor over a choreographed meal and a 'script'). Often, these donors belong to the old school; they enjoy the social cachet. They also like being part of a world that won't surprise them, and that makes them feel good about the money they give. Who can blame them?

The 'ladies who lunch' have been around forever. But consider this: the report 'Women and Million Dollar Giving: Current Landscape and Trends to Watch' found that in high-net-worth households, 84% of women are the primary decision-maker or joint decision-maker regarding investments. Women were also identified in the report as being twice as likely to view charitable giving as the most satisfying aspect of wealth, and also more likely to value their wealth as a way to create positive change.

What About Trust?

I'm not advocating for the sort of change whose big goal is to make givers happy. This is about the charitable funding of worthy causes. With breakdowns in communication and trust, such as the ones I've described, the entire sector is in trouble.

A recent Better Business Bureau study found that, although 73% of donors consider trust in organizations a prerequisite for giving, only 19% report having high levels of trust in philanthropies. The numbers don't lie: we have a serious problem.

Then there is the fact that, at last count, we've got $121B sitting in Donor Advised Funds. That this money isn't getting out to nonprofits might actually be a trust thing too. Donor Advised Funds (or DAFs, as they're known) give people many of the benefits of giving – among them, serious tax savings as well as the fulfillment of a moral imperative (assuming such an imperative exists) regarding personal philanthropy. But DAFs provide a place for donors to *put* their money; they don't actually require this money to be distributed onward to charities. So, for donors who distrust philanthropies, or those exhausted by the tactics of fundraising, DAFs are a bit of a 'hall pass.'

Organizations themselves can't afford to trust that big donors will always sustain them, although they certainly sustain them now. In 2015, the most recent year for which IRS data is available, 51.6% of charitable donations in the USA came from households with annual incomes of $100,000 and above. This was up a good 20% from the early 2000s, when giving (and, importantly, wealth) spread more equitably across the population.

It's estimated that, in the next thirty years or so, as much as $68 trillion in wealth will pass from the Baby Boomers to our younger generations – namely, Millennials. This is a mind-boggling scenario that I'll return to in the coming chapters. Suffice it to say for now that this transfer of wealth represents real opportunity for the sector, as well as significant risk. Most major charitable gifts come from donors with long-standing commitments to the organizations they support, donors who have been cultivated by fundraisers for years. So, if nonprofits don't connect meaningfully with the next generations now, they might be looking at losing them entirely. By the time they get on the bandwagon and actually speak to these younger people, it will very likely be too late.

The research shows that, no matter your age, giving small is what leads to giving big. If you're going to be a major donor at some point in your lifetime, you invariably start off with lesser gifts. Shouldn't that make us wonder how exactly the sector's old-fashioned tactics – which often focus on big gifts at the expense (or offense) of smaller donors – will attract new supporters? *My* worry is that they won't. Nonprofits will continue to rely, in the meantime, on their older, wealthier donors and these donors will, to put it bluntly, eventually die.

Then what happens? You already know the answer.

But there is hope, and that's why we're here. Millennials especially have become incredibly engaged in the public sphere, and they're demonstrating commitment to the causes that matter to them in new and exciting ways. They're also already giving at impressive rates – and those that *will* inherit through the generational handover haven't even done so yet.

THE OVERARCHING IMPACT OF NEXT-GENERATION DONORS

Here's some food for thought from *Generation Impact* authors Sharna Goldseker and Michael Moody:

'America's next generation of major donors, whether young Gen Xers or rising Millennials, will have an outsized impact on society and the planet we share, as people like Andrew Carnegie and John D. Rockefeller did in years past and as people like Bill and Melinda Gates and Warren Buffett are doing now – likely even more impact. [They] will decide which diseases get the most research funding, which environmental organizations launch the biggest awareness campaigns, which new ideas for incubation reform are incubated around the country. And those decisions will impact, directly and daily, our health, our communities, our economies, our culture, and even our climate.'

Now That's a Meeting

As something of an alien on planet philanthropy, I'm awed by what I've seen: incredible generosity on all sides, as well as a whole lot of stuff that doesn't work and that definitely doesn't support our causes. Because I care and because I've got chutzpah, I'm going to continue to call this stuff out. But I'll also propose a solution. In the coming chapters, I'll lay out a more humane approach to fundraising that's supported by research (my own, and that of others) and validated by what I've learned in business. I'll be asking nonprofits to be more upfront in their communications, more authentic in their relationships, and more transparent in their practices generally. I'll also insist that those readers who are already philanthropists work hard to create a sector that's less stratified and more focused on cause and integrity.

In the process, I hope to convince you that for every disappointing interaction in fundraising, there exists a meaningful alternative that has a bit of a snowball effect: it increases our chances of delivering measurable impact. Not only do I believe this with head and heart, I've witnessed it firsthand. And I've talked with so many funders and fundraisers whose positive stories are proof. So, as something of an antidote to all the bad news, I'm going to leave you with one last story before we move on to the next chapter. It's about an experience that keeps Josh and me going, where the sector is concerned, one that occurred very early in our lives as philanthropists.

We'd just moved into the house I described in my introduction, and I extended an invitation to visit to David Levinson. David is the founder and director of Big Sunday, an amazing nonprofit that connects people who want to volunteer or donate with other organizations that need help. We wanted to explore how Josh and I could make a significant impact in supporting our city's most needy.

Although it was our first meeting with David, it felt like the second or third. Granted, we went into it with huge admiration for Big Sunday's mission, that of harnessing absolutely everyone's instinct to give. But David also came informed. This enabled us to zoom through all the stages involved in the getting-to-know-you portion of meetings.

We knew we were aligned. We didn't need to conform to the metrics that so many organizations require (those six or seven touchpoints of cultivation, for example, which often feel to donors like 'prescribed' communications and outreach – snail mail, email, phone call, event – all designed to get us to give).

The three of us just put it all out there. 'What do you care about?' David asked.

I loved the directness of his question, and in response we discussed some of the most pressing needs in Los Angeles, where we live. These were many, what with the country still being in the fog at that time of the 2008 recession. Throughout the conversation, David was engaged, informed, and utterly reciprocal. He didn't pander, and not once did he pretend that we weren't talking about a gift.

As we were wrapping up, I put forward what I thought was a great idea. 'David,' I said, 'What if Josh and I were to feed every hungry person in Los Angeles for three months? What would it cost?'

He paused. 'Let me work on that and get back to you.'

A few weeks later he returned to our home for a follow-up meeting. Again, I asked: 'What would it cost to feed every hungry person in our city for three months?' I was convinced at that point that my idea was brilliant.

And David's response? He said, 'I'm not going to tell you.'

Then he went on. 'Lisa, it's irrelevant. It's a bad idea because it's not sustainable. You feed everyone for three months and then what? What happens in month four?'

Okay. I was listening.

David sent us a proposal after that, which included a number of workable options. Among them was something we called the 'End of the Month Club,' an initiative so named for the way it would address the high demand experienced at the end of each month by food banks, whose clients have used up all their money at that point, and need help to feed their families. The idea was to engage corporations and institutions, as well as volunteers, to ensure that the pantries would be stocked at exactly the point that the food-insecure need them.

We told David we loved the idea. At which point he gave us a number for what it would cost, assured us we could fund the requisite staffing, and we were sold.

What I appreciated about the interaction, and all the more in retrospect, is that David didn't come with prepackaged ideas, nor did he present a number that he'd determined in advance. We had a real conversation of substance. He took the time to research my idea but also came up with something better. He gave me a figure based on cost, and not our perceived 'capacity.' And, because we'd established a real connection, he was able to tell me my idea was lousy. Not only that, I was able to hear him!

And the result? The End of the Month Club, which we continue to fund, has leveraged our initial donation to the extent that it now collects and distributes many hundreds, often thousands, of food items every month. In addition to the food banks of the original proposal, these items go to nonprofits, schools, afterschool programs, senior centers, vets' centers, and any place else where people are hungry.

Also, the End of the Month Club has kickstarted multiple initiatives for Big Sunday relating to food insecurity, which together have attracted attention from supermarkets, food manufacturers, and other corporations with a desire to help. Every November, as just one example, the organization gives away more than 30,000 items as part of its popular annual Thanksgiving Stuffing Event.

That's a lot of goodness, and all of it stemming from a single, straightforward, and humane interaction between two rookie donors and a fundraiser.

Putting the Humanity Back into Fundraising

Something special happened when David engaged Josh and me as thinking, feeling people whose reasons for having the conversation in the first place were not all that different from his own. For me, it's an ideal model.

It also makes certain things clear. If organizations want to stay relevant, they're going to have to realize that what's personal in our relationships – it can't be faked. Donors see through it. And nor can the 'professional' be faked. Donors of all ages want more information about the nonprofits they support than they ever have in the past, and with good reason. We'll delve into nonprofit governance issues in Chapter Five. In the meantime, I suspect nothing I've said in this chapter is particularly earth-shattering. Our best philanthropic educators understand that change is necessary, and they've got some great advice about how to embrace it. But the clock is ticking, and while some organizations are ready or maybe even living this change already, many others are nowhere near.

In the most cynical recesses of my heart, I wonder if it's because the sector's old guard is getting ready to comfortably retire – at just about the same time as our old donors will pass. After all, if these institutional bigwigs can manage to maintain the status quo, at least for now, they won't have to deal with the hassle (as well as the enormous complexity) of guiding their organizations into the future.

Yes, innovation and change are inherently uncertain. But it's high time we did this differently, and started teaching it differently, too. There are so many development professionals out there who can't wait to deliver substantial change to the sector, but who are also very reasonably afraid that, if they don't make their targets ... well, programs get cut, employees get fired; at worse, beneficiaries suffer.

It doesn't have to be that way. In the coming chapters, I'll share more of my story, and integrate the wisdom and experiences of my peers: donors, volunteers, nonprofit professionals, and academics from the Lilly Family School of Philanthropy, the College of Civic Life at Tufts University, and elsewhere. I'll also offer actionable advice that will help chart the way forward for all of us.

Wouldn't it be great to get to a place where organizations trust donors enough to be transparent, and donors trust organizations enough to let them lead? That place is where we realize that we want the same thing: organizations that are as effective as they are visionary, and outcomes that change the world.

TWO

DONORS AND THEIR MOTIVES

The Old Rules Don't Apply

Nobody prepares you to come into money. We *flew* in, actually, on a private plane that the company sent, to take us to the New York Stock Exchange. This 'flying private' thing was a first, and our twins, who couldn't have been more than four years old, took full advantage of the gourmet spread. Then our son threw up everywhere …

I felt like the Beverly Hillbilly.

But it was really something, seeing Josh ring that bell at the 'Big Board' on Wall Street, and I guess I expected then that everything would change.

What I didn't expect is that, with certain people, the old 'me' would vanish. Those people were often fundraisers, and beginning right after the IPO, as well as in the years that followed, I'd come to meet such people in droves. That's when I started to question why the old 'me' (the woman who wasn't just a rich-lady stereotype) could exist as normal in other parts of my life, just never when it came to fundraising. It was as if this certain kind of fundraiser couldn't acknowledge that I was anything other than an ATM.

Instead of enjoying being a donor, I felt like a commodity – one of the shares on offer in Josh's IPO. I started to wonder if this uneasy feeling was my penalty for our wealth, or if fighting for the respect that I'd earned in my decades in the workplace was just what I'd have to do now, all over again, as a donor.

Granted, I've met some great people along the way, and I'm also convinced that the sector is full of them, if you look. Which is why, if I thought for a second that what I experienced worked best for philanthropy, or that I was alone in my reaction to it, I might have stayed quiet.

It *doesn't* work, however. And, it turns out, I'm not alone in my thinking.

I was reminded of this a couple of years ago on a bitterly cold day in Cambridge, Massachusetts, during a tour of Harvard that I took with my daughter. Although we'd purchased tickets from a seemingly official place in Harvard Square, I think students must have been running this particular tour, and our student guide spoke a lot about donors. He led our little group to different buildings, describing how they were named or who was behind them, and eventually he said, 'Here's a story.' Then he told us about a pair of farmers, a couple, the woman in a gingham dress and the man all proud in his oversized suit. One day, this couple showed up at the office of the Harvard president.

The office gatekeeper, a secretary, was not exactly warm. First, she tried to get them to leave, and then she made them wait for hours. In fact, not until the president emerged at the end of the day did the couple get a chance to tell him why they had come. Their son had been at Harvard! And he'd loved it. Tragically, this son had died in an accident after his freshman year, and now the couple wanted to build a memorial. To which the president, sneering somewhat, said something about Harvard not being in the business of gravestones.

The couple exchanged a look. 'No,' the man said. 'We mean a building.'

And the president laughed. 'You don't know what that costs.'

Then he told them. And Mr and Mrs Leland Stanford instead went to Palo Alto, California, to build an entire school in honor of their son, a memorial to the student that Harvard didn't care to remember.

Amazing, right? That's what I thought, too … until I learned from our guide that the story is an urban myth. Apparently, some people (our guide being one of them) enjoy this myth for its implicit lesson.

Never judge your donors by their looks.

A Cautionary Tale About Stereotypes

It turns out that Leland Stanford, once a California governor, made his fortune in business. He and his wife Jane had a son, Leland Jnr, who died of typhoid fever, but Harvard never entered the picture. 'The children of California shall be our children,' said the elder Leland to Jane, on the day of their son's death. And that was the beginning of Stanford University.

What's interesting to me is that the myth has survived, despite being debunked on the Internet and elsewhere. Obviously, there are real-life parallels. (We had to call Cedars seven times, for example, before they took us seriously as donors.) But the thing with the Stanfords of the Harvard tale is that they fit neither the stereotype of 'old' money or 'new'. There was no bling or obvious snobbery; only regular clothes and a whole lot of patience. Their money didn't 'talk,' their wealth didn't 'whisper,' and they definitely didn't look like 'they'd covered themselves in glue,' as Margaret Atwood described the nouveau riche in *The Blind Assassin*, and 'then rolled around in hundred-dollar bills.'

Honestly, I feel for these fictional Stanfords. I feel for the Vegas tycoon, William Lindsay, who saw *Brigadoon* and fell in love with Scotland (a place he'd never been), but was taken for a crank when he tried to give a massive donation to a Glasgow university. I also feel for the charities that continue to misread prospective donors, using the same old out-dated tropes in a totally new era.

Back when I worked in Hollywood, I oversaw the creation of the online divisions of NBC and Universal studios. As anyone would when scoping out new opportunities, I relied heavily on consumer research into what people wanted and why. The experience taught me a lot about motives and how feeling good – really feeling human and connected – drives us.

Donors want to feel human and connected too. That's only natural. But donors have changed, often in ways we don't realize. And if charities continue to operate under the same old assumptions, their attempts at connection will fail.

If you look at me and see an archetype, I can tell. I can see it in the restaurant you've picked for our meeting, or the tone of your voice on the phone – especially how your voice rises in pitch about three seconds in, the moment I say: 'This is Lisa.' I'm not fancy like that, and I don't need your deference.

I'm also closer to the rule, in terms of background, than the exception. A 2017 study from Fidelity Investments found that 88% of millionaires are self-made. Add to that fact the almost viral manner in which newcomers to this group are multiplying, and you begin to see how philanthropy's old-money tactics are, well, old.

A NEW BILLIONAIRE EVERY TWO DAYS

That astonishing fact – a new billionaire every two days – comes directly from *Forbes* magazine. In 2018, 195 new billionaires were minted; among them, In-N-Out Burger heiress Lynsi Snyder and Spotify's Daniel Ek. Of this newcomer group, 34% made their fortunes in technology.

Scale down about a thousand million, and you'll see that people with wealth are getting younger. As Chicago-based research firm Spectrem reported, the average age of US investors with $25M or more has dropped by eleven years since 2014 – to forty-seven!

Then there are the regular millionaires. Credit Suisse's latest global wealth report shows that in mid 2019, there were 46.8 million millionaires (calculated in USD) world-wide, an increase of 1.1 million from 2018.

Many new millionaires are also disruptors – that's how they've come to success in the first place. And that impulse to move, to be quick and to buck convention, it's going to play out in their giving. I was driving down the freeway recently when I saw a billboard ad for Soylent. I couldn't believe it. Like its namesake in the movie *Soylent Green*, a dystopian thriller from the seventies, the product on that billboard is a meal replacement. It's super popular, apparently, at tech companies in Silicon Valley, where people drink it at their desks when they don't have time for lunch.

Are these our new donors, these imbibers of Soylent?

Given the wealth that's being amassed by tech-sector workers (and what it would mean, to charities, to get a piece of that wealth), I certainly hope so.

'It's Wiser to Find Out than Suppose'

Mark Twain said it first – 'It's wiser to find out than suppose' – and he's right, even (or especially!) in fundraising. If you work at a charity, finding out what motivates donors is critical to the success of your cause. Only, as I've been explaining, the conventional wisdom in the sector is based entirely on suppositions.

Such as: *Donors are motivated by guilt.*

And: *Donors like to be coddled, ideally over a very long lunch.*

And: *Adult donors were trust-fund kids. They have no business sense, and little common sense. While they like shiny things, they themselves are not that bright.*

I could go on.

This is less about what motivates us to give than it is about what gets us to open our purse strings. And that's a shame, because donors are people, and, like all people, our drives and desires reflect the million different experiences that define us as individuals. This includes what inspires us philanthropically. If my friend Jen is drinking Soylent – or let's say she *used* to drink Soylent during the amassing of her fortune – she'd prob-ably rather stick forks in her eyeballs than have to sit through a two-hour lunch. Still, charities need to connect with Jen and people like her.

In its hidebound approach to prospects, the sector's failure to distinguish between those who have inherited their money and those who have earned it is just the tip of the iceberg. I was doing some research on this recently and found an Indiana University Centre on Philanthropy study from more than a decade ago. My guess is that not only are its recommendations still being used by fundraisers today, they've been used by fundraisers for the last half-century! It's about segmenting, with the study classifying donors according to income, education, and geography, and then issuing pitch strategies based on those classifications.

How reductive, that the sector's educators are encouraging fundraisers to subscribe to false assumptions about prospective donors. And how utterly fake, the idea that fundraisers should change their behavior depending on the 'category' of the prospect.

Believe it or not, here are the study's main recommendations:

1. When approaching people with an income of less than $100,000, or those with high-school education or less: emphasize how your organization helps people meet their basic needs or helps people help themselves.

2. When approaching prospective donors with an income of $100,000 or more, or those with a college degree or above: emphasize how their gift helps them help those with less (for equity). Demonstrate how your organization can 'help make the world a better place' or, if more appropriate, help make the community better.

This is a great example of what's wrong with the practice of philanthropy. The recommendations assume that people – prospective donors – who don't have a college degree *or* make less than $100,000 per year (equivalent to $127,000 per year in today's dollars) have completely different motivations for giving, as well as different ways of expressing their interest in giving, than those who do have degrees or make more money.

The first offence, as I see it, is in the subtext. Prospects in the 'have degree/have money' category are considered more valuable – worthy of the time it takes an organization to 'demonstrate' as opposed to 'emphasize.' Then there's the fact that the recommendations seem to virtually ignore the many hugely successful people without college degrees.

Shall I go on? Think about teachers, who typically earn less than $127,000 per year. The recommendations appear to suggest that they're incapable of engaging in a conversation about giving as it relates to equity and community and bettering the world (as opposed to helping people 'meet their basic needs'). We're talking about the capacity for thinking strategically as well as tactically – an ability that is not unique to the rich. And speaking of the rich, this approach leaves no room whatsoever for the millions of people in tech (as one example among many), who make modest salaries but have valuable stock in their companies.

Approaching me with the 'make the world a better place' thing because you think I can't relate to the 'help people help themselves' thing creates rules of engagement that have nothing to do with me, the donor, or you, the fundraiser. Let alone the cause.

We've Got Trust Issues

That same Indiana University study makes the excellent point that, societally, a higher level of *general* trust is associated with more confidence in charitable organizations. Our problem today is that institutional trust is in recession.

Globally, according to the 2019 Edelman Trust Barometer, only 56% of people trust NGOs. It's worse in the USA (at 52%), bottoming out in the UK (at 47%), and is just slightly healthier in Canada (at 59%). Edelman, which has been tracking this stuff for almost twenty years, reported a striking nine-point decline in trust in NGOs between 2017 and 2018 alone. What people appear to be doing as a result is shifting their trust to relationships within their control, most notably their employers. This may well explain the growing appetite out there for impact investing – but we'll get into that later in the chapter.

In the meantime, let's not kid ourselves. Unless we change the old rules of engagement, which themselves are institutional relics, we're going to continue to bump into this problem of trust. If those of us with the capacity to give don't trust our institutions to do right with our money, the bottom falls out of the whole concept. It's one of the reasons I'm specifically putting donors and fundraisers in the hot seat, leaving foundations for a future discussion. This is about people over systems.

TRUST WORKS BOTH WAYS:
BEWARE OF ULTERIOR MOTIVES

I was once involved with the operations of a particular nonprofit when we got an unsolicited call from a community member. This person wanted to fund the creation of a garden in front of our facility. Although it had never occurred to us to create a garden, we thought it was a nice gesture. Since the donor wanted us to begin work on the garden more or less immediately, we readily agreed to a further conversation. And that's when we learned that the donation came with strings attached – namely, that we agree to promote the gift with the donor's name and also let the donor promote the donation himself in whatever way he wished.

After a bit of research, we discovered that the prospective donor was involved in some pretty heavy legal issues and was facing a jail sentence. Knowing that we were just a pawn in this guy's scheme and knowing, too, that we needed his money to reach our targets, should we have said no? That's a question for Chapter Six, where we'll get into issues of ethics and trust. The point here is that this kind of scenario isn't unique – and we all need to watch out for it.

Since that experience, I've heard plenty of stories about donors using generosity as a tactic – usually when they've got court dates looming. Not okay.

Religious Guilt Is Getting Old

I'm going to get personal for a minute and talk about the way religious guilt works in the Jewish community. The answer to the question of why people within the Jewish community give, the uber answer, has always been … Holocaust guilt. One hundred percent of the time.

It's obligation over generosity, and guilt even more than obligation. It's also supposed to 'hurt', in the sense that we're asked to give a little more than we may think we're comfortable giving, which is something I'll return to in Chapter Seven. Suffice it to say for now that what is often implied (if not outright stated) when I'm approached is, 'We want it to hurt.' And 'It's not enough if it doesn't hurt.'

In considering motives, the issue becomes one of whether these organizations are right in this belief, in this day and age, that donors actually want to hurt themselves. That's over, in my view. It doesn't work. I won't speak to the parallels that exist in the world's other major religions and their various faith-based forms of philanthropy. But I do know that they exist.

What I will say is that, if guilt is on its way out, so far as my generation goes, how is it possibly going to engage even younger donors? People of all ages still do give to causes the reports classify as 'worship'. But the number of backsides on the seats (or on the floor or the carpets) of churches, synagogues, temples, and mosques is at an all-time low. And if these religious institutions continue to pander to their legacy donors, who may well respond to guilt but who won't be around forever, they're going to be left with empty places of worship and even emptier coffers.

It's happening already. For example, a large Jewish nonprofit I know refused to send a bus to help transport people to the 2017 Los Angeles Women's March, which recorded crowds of approximately 750,000. Why? Because someone in the organization worried about offending a couple of donors. Hundreds of people – particularly young people, whom the organization is dying to attract – would have appreciated this bus. For them, the bus would have looked like a gesture of trust and maybe even support of a more progressive approach, making them far more likely to extend *their* support to the nonprofit. Still, no bus.

It's happening.

FEWER NEW DONORS MOTIVATED TO GIVE

Chapter One looked at how giving is increasing, but only because of larger gifts from richer donors. Cue a recent study by the Fundraising Effectiveness Project, which tracked the results of more than 4,500 American nonprofits. It found that the number of people who gave in 2018 fell by 4.5%, while the landing of new donors fell by 7.3%. *Nonprofit Quarterly* unpacked the report with Ben Miller (whose firm is behind it) and he issued a warning – not only about the impact of the results on smaller nonprofits with fewer connections to wealth, but also the survival of the sector. 'From past reports,' he said, 'we've seen that charities seemed to do well at acquiring new donors but retaining them was a challenge. Now we're seeing difficulties in acquiring donors, and that could spell real trouble.' (For more on donor retention, see Chapter Seven.)

What Miller isn't saying is that the landscape has changed. Why people give and how they feel about impact, equity or accountability; even how they made their money – this has all changed. And as they say, adapt or die.

The Truth About Tax-Advantaged Giving

You might think my contention is that all donors are fresh-faced, pure of heart, and just dying to get on the right bus. I'm afraid this isn't so.

Even those who give generously sometimes reveal their motives in somewhat disappointing ways. Donor Advised Funds, while amazing in many respects, also offer us a lens into what can happen when donors have an incentive (in the form of a tax break) but lack inspiration. Or, as I explained in Chapter One, when their motives for giving are less than ideal.

As you're no doubt aware, many consider Donor Advised Funds *the* charitable vehicle of choice. We'll discuss how charities can tap into DAFs later, but it's important to explore first why the term 'charitable vehicle' is fraught.

The amount of money sitting in DAFs is staggering. At the end of 2019, Bloomberg put the total at $121 billion. When the 2019 Giving USA report published its findings for 2018, it estimated that there was at least $110 billion sitting in DAFs in the USA alone – a figure that was in the high $90-billion range just a year earlier. These totals are obviously testament to the exponential rate of the growth of these funds. DAFs were created decades ago but became super popular in the 1980s and 1990s, and even more so in recent years.

MILLENNIALS USING TECH STOCK TO INVEST IN CHARITY

Donor Advised Funds typically include contributions of non-cash assets, such as stock, company shares, and real estate. Schwab Charitable, for example, which has a minimum DAF account balance of $5,000, to encourage a diversity of donors, reports that its 2019 contributions were up 30% over the previous fiscal year. Schwab also reports that, as Millennials transfer some of their assets to DAFS –

with non-cash assets (including tech stocks) making up roughly two-thirds of their DAF contributions – they're also averaging six grants per year of $4,000 each.

That DAFs are called 'charitable vehicles' is a tad misleading, mind you, in that charities aren't seeing a whole lot of that pile of DAF money. It's estimated that between 5 and 20% (the Institute for Policy Studies' figure was higher than other stats I've seen) is actually getting passed on to any kind of charitable organization annually. Some of the money is in community foundations, where a portion of the fees (fees that themselves are a percentage of the balance in the fund!) goes back to the community – a very good thing. But most of it sits in the big financial institutions that have created these funds for their clients. Yes, the organizations housing and managing the funds are charitable in their own right, otherwise the DAF wouldn't work, but, for the most part, the funds sit there until the donor, who retains advisory privileges, decides where the money should go. How long before the money has to be transferred to a charity? Legally, as long as you want. A month, a year, a decade, *more* – all kosher in the world of DAFs.

This might be okay if a donor, for the sake of argument, has come into money suddenly, and wants to take time to do some research and apportion it thoughtfully. This is a perfectly reasonable use of a DAF. But letting money sit because you don't want to deal with it is a problem. Maybe you don't want to deal with the fundraisers – the pitches, calls, lunches, and so on. Maybe you also know that, when giving to an organization via a DAF, your name is often on the check or transfer, which means that you then have to manage the ongoing pressure to donate to that organization again. (We'll get into donor communications strategies in Chapter Seven.) My point for now is that many prospective donors just don't want to enter the slipstream. So it's better to take the tax deduction and let the money (the amount of which is undisclosed, typically, remaining anonymous until it's dispersed to charity) flow only when you're ready.

For the truly charitable donors among us, DAFs are a double-edged sword in that the institutions that house them have zero motivation to help us choose which charities to support. Remember, the fees these institutions get are a percentage of the balance in DAF accounts, which arguably curtails their motivation to disperse the money.

Ka-ching!

When I was first participating in a DAF program, I couldn't understand why the foundation that housed the program wasn't emailing me almost weekly to tell me about all the great charities to which I could direct my money. I even sent a list of my favorites to this foundation, thinking that its staff members would function as matchmakers – cupid-like conduits between donor and charity. Turns out I was being naive.

The Institute for Policy Studies is advocating for a reform in the rules governing DAFs to require distribution of DAF donations within three years. That's a hugely positive step in the right direction. And, in fact, DAFs have lots of positives, if used as intended. For example, mine lets me access an overview of when and how my charitable dollars have been spent, quickly donate whenever I want, separate individual gifts from the tax deductions associated with them, and ensure a small percentage of fees go to a cause that matters – in this case, the foundation where my DAF is housed. It's also super easy to contribute to, so much so that I set up DAFs for our kids, the twins, when they were five years old.

Finally, a Generation That Won't Stay in Its Lane

Did I mention kids? By the time this book goes to press, our oldest Millennials – at least according to the folks who put that generation's start date at 1980 – will be forty. So, where do we get off thinking that *any* of them want to sit at the kids' table? Sure, they might look, behave, and even give differently than the generations before them, but enough with the ageism that's so rampant in the sector. They're adults. And along with Gen Y, they've got a huge role to play in 'saving giving' (or #SavingGiving, for those interested in finding me on Twitter using the hashtag that, to me, really underscores why we're here).

I want to be careful not to generalize in a chapter about resisting assumptions. Millennials are as variable in their passions as other generations, but they're also showing a tendency to care about issues over institutions. The 2019 Millennial Impact Report, which reflects the largest body of data and analysis on how American Millennials interact with causes, tells us that more than 90% of Millennials would stop giving to an organization if they began to distrust it. And three-quarters would stop giving if they weren't told how their contributions help.

This is critical information, which reinforces all the talk recently about 'impact investing'. The Korn Ferry Institute (a global consulting firm specializing in organizational strategy) and others, for example, have reported on a trend toward *integration* in our expression of values. If I care (and I do care, deeply) about issues relating to girls and women, I probably won't want to simply write a check to a related cause and then forget about it. Maybe I'll still write that check to a charity that supports girls and women, but I'll also invest in like-minded companies. Or I'll choose products that reflect my values – for example, clothing that isn't made in a sweatshop, where 90% of laborers are girls and women.

If I were just coming up in the world, according to Korn Ferry, my attitudes toward work and money would be different too, with the result being incredibly hopeful, i.e. 'the rise in responsible and sustainable environmental, social and governance practices as a business imperative.'

I see it in the social consciousness of my oldest kids, who are Millennials, especially with respect to how they donate and their views on impact investing. It's through them that I was introduced to Resource Generation. With fifteen chapters across the USA, this is an organization for people thirty-five and under who are committed, through their giving behavior and otherwise, to a redistribution of the power that comes with money.

Chapter leader Andrea Pien's family has a Donor Advised Fund, but, she tells me, 'Being involved with Resource Generation has helped me think more deeply about how I give and how the giving relationship is cultivated with grantees.' We'll return to Andrea in Chapter Three, when we discuss some of the ways she and other Resource Generation members are empowering those affected by their grant-making. In the meantime, Andrea's perspective is important to this conversation about motives:

> I'm Chinese-American and, prior to Resource Generation, I'd never met any other young people of color with wealth besides my sister. Going to college made me more politicized and that's when I started thinking about issues of race and gender and social justice. But I didn't really do any in-depth work around class. Now I'm in education and I see wealth inequality very visibly. I think understanding that, *yes*, we (as in, young people of color with wealth) work hard, but we also have some unearned privilege – this makes it easier for us to let go of the need to be controlling about the money we do have.

THE GREAT WEALTH
TRANSFER

$68 trillion in wealth held by 45 million US households will
transfer from one generation to the next in the coming
twenty-five to thirty years

$15 trillion in global wealth will move from one generation
to the next in the coming ten years

$8.8 trillion will transfer generations in North America
during the same period, much of it in the USA

$3.2 trillion will transfer generations in Europe, reflecting
the region's slightly older wealthy class

$1.9 trillion will transfer in Asia, in this case because the
region's wealthy are substantially younger

YCore is another organization that, in its own words, 'mobilizes young professionals to advance community-based social impact by teaching them to deploy their time, money, skills, and influence as partners and advocates.' Kana Hammon, who is YCore's co-founder and executive director, has spoken to me about not actually coming from significant wealth. 'One time I was reading *Vogue* magazine,' she explains, 'and somebody profiled was a philanthropist. I thought, that's so cool. How do I become a philanthropist? And my mom was like, "You have to be really wealthy."'

In other words, wealth first; philanthropy later. And *only* later if you're hugely rich.

Kana describes YCore as a 'social impact bootcamp for young professionals,' many of whom are very early philanthropists. She says, 'Traditional philanthropy is about giving back, and is very donor-centric in that it's about what a donor can accomplish in order to feel good. I'm here to fix problems.'

I take Kana's point about traditional philanthropy, just as I admire the work that she and others are doing to create new cultures of advocacy and giving. *My* take is that what gets us to 'good,' or feeling 'good,' is highly individual. It's as different for a couple I know in their nineties, who have been giving modestly for fifty years, as it is for the self-made son of a friend, who is totally overwhelmed by his sudden fortune.

I *do* want to feel good about being a donor. But if there is a window here to get people into giving, I also want to make the most of it. No more bad experiences or missed opportunities. I want philanthropy to win.

HOW GENERATIONS DIFFER IN THEIR GIVING

A 2018 report from the Blackbaud Institute for Philanthropic Impact looks at giving demographics across the globe. Here's the US breakdown:

The Greatest

78% give • 23.5M donors • $1,235 yr./avg. • 6.3 charities •
   $29.0 billion/yr.

Support worship, local social service, emergency relief, health, children, military, formal education, the arts, and election campaigns

Baby Boomers

75% give • 55.3M donors • $1,061 yr./avg. • 4.2 charities •
   $58.6 billion/yr.

Are especially concerned with financial-accountability and support local social service, worship, health, emergency relief, children, military, and animals

Generation X

55% give • 35.8M donors • $921 yr./avg. • 3.8 charities •
   $32.9 billion/yr.

Are especially concerned with impact and support many of the causes Boomers do, with an emphasis on health services, animal rights, and environmental protection

Millennials

51% give • 34.1M donors • $591 yr./avg. • 3.5 charities •
   $20.1 billion/yr.

Are especially concerned with impact and support many of the causes Boomers do, with an emphasis on human rights, child development, and victims of abuse and crime

Generation Z

44% give • 9.3M donors • $341 yr./avg. • 4.6 charities •
   $3.2 billion/yr.

Are especially concerned with impact to the extent that 1 in 10 want to start a charity themselves

It might surprise you to know that in the UK, according to Blackbaud, Gen Z and Millennials together gave £2.7 billion [approximately $3.5 billion USD] in the twelve months studied, which was 30% of total overall donations. What's more, 40% of them intended to increase their giving amount the following year – more than double that of other generations.

Not so surprising is the fact that adults are more likely to give to charity if their parents gave to charity (Indiana University Lilly Family School of Philanthropy).

WHERE WE'RE DIRECTING OUR CHARITABLE DOLLARS

•

All numbers based on Giving USA 2019 estimates for the previous year:

– **Giving to religion** declined by 1.5% in 2018 (a decrease of 3.9% adjusted for inflation), to $124.52 billion

- **Giving to education** declined by 1.3% (decreasing 3.7% adjusted for inflation), to $58.72 billion
= **Giving to human services** stayed relatively flat, decreasing by 0.3% (a decrease of 2.7% adjusted for inflation), to $51.54 billion
- **Giving to foundations** decreased by 6.9% (declining by 9.1% adjusted for inflation) to $50.29 billion, based on data provided by Candid
= **Giving to health organizations** had flat growth of 0.1% (a decline of 2.3% adjusted for inflation) at $40.78 billion
- **Giving to public society benefit organizations** decreased by 3.7% (decreasing 6.0% adjusted for inflation), to $31.21 billion
= **Giving to arts, culture, and humanities** stayed relatively flat, increasing 0.3% (declining 2.1% adjusted for inflation) to $19.49 billion
+ **Giving to international affairs** increased by 9.6% (an increase of 7.0% adjusted for inflation), to $22.88 billion
+ **Giving to environment and animal organizations** increased by 3.6% (an increase of 1.2% adjusted for inflation), to $12.70 billion.

It's About Checking Assumptions

Never assume anything. That's the real moral of this story. When development people assume that all they need to do is communicate the importance of a cause and I'll somehow 'get it' – maybe because they also assume that I lack direction – well, it's insulting. I mean, it's always possible to find a love match in terms of priorities, but you might as well be saying, as just one example, 'I'm the philharmonic and I need money, and whether or not you like the philharmonic, you *do* have money, so you need to give it to me.'

This actually happened to me. And what I couldn't help but think during the call is that I'm not into orchestras, so I'm not going to fund one. I'm very into the arts, and I might fund a theater, but classical music just isn't my thing.

Also, why are you calling me *again*?

A 'Five-Minute Google Search' (see pages 108–9) would have unearthed enough about my interests to save everyone some time. And, sure, I'm aware of the criticism of donors whose philanthropic interests are considered self-serving or even indulgent. This is a charge levelled at tech entrepreneurs especially, whose high-risk coupling of charity and innovation is said to be all about them, or the industries that made them, and not so much about actual need.

But Josh is a tech entrepreneur. Josh also has Crohn's. As I explained in my introduction, it's important to him to do what he can to ensure no other kids have to suffer like he did. In fact, it's exactly this desire of his, together with his experience as an innovator, which makes the IBD program at Cedars such a wonderful match.

Josh understands from personal experience that innovators do best when there's room for discovery. Here's what Dr. Dermot McGovern, the Joshua L. and Lisa Z. Greer Chair in Inflammatory Bowel Disease Genetics, had to say about it when I spoke to him:

> Our lab is funded largely through foundations or the NIH. It's incredibly competitive, which is a positive in the sense that good science is funded. But it does make things difficult, particularly if you don't have preliminary data. It also makes people conservative. What's different about the money from Lisa and Josh is that it comes without strings attached in terms of research. This allows me to do two things. First, I can generate the preliminary data I need to apply for funding from the NIH. And second, I can take on projects or adopt strategies that are high risk and high reward.

I suspect that no one at Cedars anticipated this when Josh and I – virtual unknowns in fundraising circles – first expressed an interest in becoming donors. And that's my point.

We're in This Together

None of this matters unless we connect, which is why I'll be focusing on the dynamics of our relationships in the next chapter. One of the people you'll get to know in the coming pages is Felice Mancini. She's a friend and a great example of so many things, including the assumptions *I* bring to the table.

As the daughter of Oscar-winning composer Henry Mancini and vocalist and philanthropist Ginny Mancini, Felice was probably always on track to work in music herself. Felice is also a fundraiser. She's been involved for more than two decades with the Mr. Holland's Opus Foundation, taking over as its executive director in 1998. Composer Michael Kamen scored the movie of the same name, and later started the foundation as a means of getting instruments to kids who wanted to play in school bands but couldn't afford the expense.

The thing that's relevant here is what you *wouldn't* expect. When researching this book, I almost didn't bother to ask Felice what motivated her to move into fundraising, assuming (as I'm sure anyone would) that it was surely music – her famous dad, her singer mom, or her own career as a vocalist and songwriter.

This was her response:

Remember the LA riots? There was a curfew during the riots, and fires that I could see from my house. It was really scary. I was born and raised in LA and I love the place, and I just remember thinking: I don't want to be afraid to live in my own city.

I had a friend I used to sing with, and he'd started a youth center down in the Rampart. I think because I didn't want to be afraid during the riots, I decided I'd volunteer there. The organization was in a church, but the church was in a hotspot (meaning, there were gangs in the area). And I did start volunteering, making lunch for the kids, because I wanted to put myself in the middle of a population that we only see – at least for the most part. After that I kept volunteering, and my friend asked me if I'd join the board. One thing led to another, and here I am.

Who would have thought?

THREE

FAKE FRIENDS AND UNEQUAL POWER

How to Connect When it's Complicated

Let's say you, the fundraiser, withdraw one of the assumptions I described in the previous chapter. For example, that I'm ignorant. Once you do this, the odds we have of connecting improve immediately.

Why? Because of respect. Maybe now you'll be willing to give me the benefit of the doubt, and I'll respond in kind. Or maybe we'll just talk like regular people, finally accepting the fact that a friendship can't be faked.

I'm implicated in the equation too, of course. I'm still chuckling seven years later about my very first visit to a blow-dry bar. These establishments were somewhat new to LA at the time and I was also new to navigating everyday relationships – the sort you might have with your hairdresser – as a person with money. I've always been open and friendly. I really enjoy talking to people, and the lovely woman doing my blowout was no exception. One of the first things she asked me was, 'How much time do you have?' And I said, 'Well, I've got to get home because I've got someone coming.'

I elaborated, probably under my breath: 'It's a service man.' And then I started laughing. You see, I just couldn't say that an *elevator repair man* was coming. Because what kind of person has an elevator in her house?!

My point is that I'm well aware that, as a donor who is advocating for authenticity, I too need to 'walk the talk.' There is a lot of criticism out there about donors behaving badly, and I'll tell you some stories to that effect in Chapter Five. For now, know that nobody is saying this is going to be easy.

Also worth mentioning, before we dive in, is another, recurring criticism of this sector – the one that assumes philanthropy is an exercise of power, basically the wielding of public influence by way of the 'charitable' distribution of private funds. This book's aim is to start a very different conversation (at least for the most part; see pages 102–5 and 206–8). Wealth inequality obviously exists, as do unjust imbalances of power. But the criticism – what some now call 'toxic philanthropy' – isn't exactly new. The formation of the great foundations of the Gilded Age (those created by Rockefeller and Carnegie, especially) was hugely controversial too.

As I see it, there's a chance here for everyone to have a hand in 'saving giving.' Because, in the middle of this mess, and all these troubles with the sector, lies opportunity.

MONEY IS MESSY

Quelle surprise! Money is the second leading cause of divorce in American marriages (behind infidelity) and money is the primary stressor in relationships that work. But did you also know that, according to a recent study by Bank of America, 53% of people said they'd seen a *friend-ship* end over money?

'The real issue is not money itself, but the power money gives you,' explains Princeton University sociologist Dalton Conley, in his widely quoted take on why the dynamic is so challenging. 'Money makes explicit the inequalities in a relationship, so we work hard to minimize it as a form of tact.'

What Conley's saying here, which surely hits a nerve with all of us, is that money is power in relationships, and so talking about money is taboo. In fact, it's such an issue that we pretend it *isn't* an issue. Which we call tact.

That's pretty terrible, especially when you realize that *not* talking about money will cause a stressed relationship to fail. But there is a silver lining that I'm convinced is applicable to the charitable sector: talking works. According to a recent survey by Ramsey Solutions, couples who say they have a 'great' marriage are almost twice as likely to talk about money daily or weekly, compared to those who say their marriage is 'okay' or 'in crisis'.

So, the lesson as I see it is twofold: first, let's give

ourselves a break – what we're doing isn't easy. And second? Let's be honest with one another about the transactional portion of these relationships. No more fake friendships.

So, What Are We?

That's the million-dollar question – what are we? On the one hand, the fundraisers and I are friends: we're people having lunch, and God forbid we talk about money. On the other, I've got something they want.

We're going to get into how to handle 'the ask' in Chapter Four. In the meantime, I'd like to consider what 'relationship' means in the context of charitable giving, where obvious power imbalances exist and where, too, does baggage, snobbery and other challenges.

I come from a world where sitting with someone over a meal, spending an hour-and-a-half discussing family or friends or debating politics, usually means this person is a friend. But in the bizarre world of philanthropy, Josh and I learned the hard way that what used to signify friendship often, *now*, means someone wants money.

When I'm at the end of what I think is a social call or a lovely dinner, and out of nowhere, there it comes: an ask for money … I can't help it. I feel hurt.

Then, when I'm in my own home – let's say I'm hosting a party – and I hear the whispered voice of a stranger behind me

('Introduce me to Lisa. I need to interact with Lisa.'), I frankly feel like I need a shower.

None of this is good.

But, look, I've seen the other side. At events, I've observed people who volunteer at nonprofits squandering great opportunities to talk about them. For example, a board member will fail to make a potentially valuable introduction, usually because there's an existing relationship at play that the person doesn't want to jeopardize. All I can think is that, as a board member, you're not doing your job. You've just missed a fabulous opportunity to connect a brand-new person to the organization you serve.

Years ago, a dear colleague of mine who had recently divorced said this about the perils of dating: 'I've decided to assume these guys are bad until they give me some reason to trust them. Otherwise, I'll just get hurt.' Naturally, I had an opinion about it. 'That's where we're different,' she shot back. 'You give people chances and then you get screwed.' I had to rush off to a meeting, but later I started thinking that, if this were true in dating, then it must also be true everywhere else. I returned to her office. 'It may be fine for you,' I said, taking up the conversation again. 'It isn't for me. I don't want to live that way. I'd never get the chance to know new people.'

As you can see, little has changed. I still refuse to enter relationships with my guard up, because I want to give them a fighting chance. But does that chance even exist in fundraising?

I asked this question of Timothy Seiler, who is the Rosso Fellow in Philanthropic Fundraising/Clinical Professor of

Philanthropic Studies in the Lilly Family School of Philanthropy at Indiana University. Speaking for fundraisers, he says, 'The ideal is that you'd have a relationship with every donor. The reality is, it falls short. It's more satisfying to feel that there's respect and honor and trust between donor and fundraiser, but fundraisers typically have large numbers of donors to interact with, and they just can't reach that level of sophistication with everyone.'

As is always the case, relationships grow and transform. And that, according to Timothy, requires trust. But he's optimistic, particularly when organizations take a donor-centered approach that has them fundraising not from a place of 'would you make this gift?' but rather 'what can we do to help you realize your philanthropic ambitions?'

I can hear it already – yes, *but* – because the realities of the sector are hard to ignore. Please stay with me. Here, and in the coming chapters, we're going to examine those realities with a view to big change.

UNTHINKABLE: OUR INTRO TO 'POWER' AND 'POSITION'

To celebrate after the IPO, we planned a once-in-a-lifetime cruise aboard a private yacht that would take us from Greece to the UK. My older kids weren't interested in a family trip, so we took the twins (who were five years old at the time) and Josh's parents, as well as some friends. When we picked up the yacht in Rhodes, we could hardly contain ourselves: it was incredible, like nothing we'd ever experienced. Also incredible was the staff, who immediately put us at ease.

First, we'd visit my uncle. Years ago, this uncle had decided to escape the horrors of capitalism by moving to the remote Greek island of Ikaria, where he lives off the land. With this part of our itinerary settled, we departed the next morning from Rhodes. Only, as we left the harbor, the yacht really lurched, toppling a vase in our stateroom.

The crew told us everything was fine, but I had a feeling over the course of that day and into the evening that the crew's behavior wasn't normal. I finally convinced the captain to tell me why. It turns out that when the ship had lurched so dramatically, the chef – preparing lobster below deck – had been scalded by a massive pot of boiling water, resulting in burns to both of his feet. While the chef had insisted, despite his pain, that he work through the injury, it was becoming increasingly clear that the burns were serious. The poor man needed a hospital.

'Oh my God,' I said. 'Let's get him to a hospital! Why didn't you tell us immediately?'

Apparently, the captain hadn't wanted it to ruin our day. He went on to explain that the only reason he was 'troubling' me with the information at all was to 'warn' me that we wouldn't be able to eat dinner on the yacht that night. We'd have to make arrangements in Rhodes. Over and over again, he apologized for the 'inconvenience,' the 'improper' dinner we'd be forced to eat at port, and the 'offence.'

The offence?!

Unfortunately, it gets worse. When the chef appeared later, ready to disembark, he was wearing heavy shoes on his two burned feet. Again, I found the captain. 'Why is the chef wearing shoes?'

It seems the chef was embarrassed. 'He didn't feel it right,' the captain said, 'that you should be subjected to his feet.'

I still remember the look we shared – Josh and me – when we understood how much the crew had tried to spare us. Or worse, 'protect' us (with someone's health in the balance), and only because we were rich. What kind of terrible world had we entered?

So Many Masters, So Little Respect

The bottom line is the bottom line. That's how my friend Sheila describes one of fundraising's basic truths. Sheila is a development director, and she makes the important point that, above all else, fundraisers are accountable to a boss and a set of numbers. They're loyal to the organization, they're accountable as employees – and this makes their friendships with donors a challenge.

Fundraising is sales, in Sheila's view, and though I feel I have to put in a word here for passion and cause, I do respect where she's coming from. It's a world in which everything, from cold calls and donor visits to actual relationships, is quantified. We're talking return on investment per *hour*. For this reason and others, Sheila worries when development officers 'work too much on the personal.' Maybe they're less focused, as a result, on 'moving the relationship forward,' or their boundary-crossing friendship with a donor raises the issue of ethics. In the case of the latter, this could be because a donor has disclosed something regarding future plans or family that the fundraiser can know, but not the charity.

Then there's the churn of turnover. Among fundraisers, as I noted in Chapter One, the average stint at a given organization is sixteen to eighteen months. And that's on a good day. Yet relationships take time to develop. So, you've got someone who's under pressure to please their boss, meet their targets, *and* build relationships – often with donors who are bossy, and busy, themselves. No wonder people burn out.

Sheila thinks it's a lot for any professional to handle, let alone someone who's relatively young. And the truth is, many development officers *are* young. In addition, 'if you're a person of color in your thirties,' she explains, 'and you're asking an old white guy for money, it can trigger feelings related to race, gender, and class. It can also be intimidating.'

I've spoken with many in the sector who agree, although some are less intimidated than they are totally fed up with the dynamics at play. These are the ones who run screaming. One such former fundraiser, still only in his twenties, is Rick. He admits that a lot of his colleagues are getting to the point where they say, 'Screw this. I'm smart, educated, and skilled. I don't mind paying my dues, but I *chose* development. And I don't want to deal with the impossible goals. I definitely don't want to deal with the condescension.'

If compensation were better, would the situation improve? *I* think so, because pay is an issue, too – one that many sector leaders are afraid to discuss. We'll talk about raising money for operations in Chapter Four. In the meantime, I'm reminded of a conversation I once had with a guy who sits on the board of a major UK charity. We were discussing how transparency makes us vulnerable to criticism, and we were also discussing pay.

This respected senior board member spoke about how pay structures make retention a challenge, not to mention recruitment. And he told me the story of a now-famous TED Talk. It featured Dan Pallotta, whose for-profit firm, Pallotta Team Works, produced the sector's successful AIDs Rides and Avon Walk for Breast Cancer, among other blockbuster charity events. In the TED Talk (which has now been viewed nearly five million times), Pallotta urges the sector to adopt a corporate model, and start paying the high-end professionals who work for nonprofits exactly what they're worth.

'Can you guess what happened to him in response?' asked my board-member acquaintance.

Apparently, in charitable circles, Pallotta was skewered. In fact, *The New York Times* would eventually call him 'one of the most controversial figures in the nonprofit sector,' and I'm not altogether surprised. I still encounter people who think development professionals should work for free, or else subscribe to an 'unwritten code' about overhead (and overhead spending) that, as I've mentioned, I'll return to later.

In the meantime, here's how Pallotta himself describes his encounters with this 'code' in his book, *Uncharitable: How Restraints on Nonprofits Undermine Their Potential*:

For example, after explaining to a friend that we need to let charities hire the most talented people in the world, he whole-heartedly agreed and then said something that didn't logically follow: "It makes me angry to see people making high salaries in charities." Even if they're worth it? Why? I asked. "Because it's supposed to be nonprofit," he replied. Right there he gave expression to the entire problem. His logic was internally consistent but externally nonsensical. Still, I understood where he was coming from. Twenty years ago I felt the same way. In fact, I remember thinking it was unconscionable that a charity event producer I knew was making a profit "off of," as I thought of it at the time, people's compassion. "Nonprofit" means you don't seek gain for yourself. So when someone wants a high salary, of course it makes us angry. It is a violation of the fundamental basis of the system.

ANOTHER UNWRITTEN CODE:
NEVER SPEAK TRUTH TO POWER

It's hard to forget what came to light in 2019 about the now-deceased predator Jeffrey Epstein – how, for decades, he engaged in criminal acts, mostly with impunity. Other truths have also surfaced, and with them a warning for those involved in philanthropy.

Much has been said about Epstein's fortune, with many wondering if it existed at all. That a high-school teacher who went on to spend five years at Bear Stearns before being let go for financial irregularities also claimed to be a billionaire is certainly odd. But what are the lessons here for nonprofits?

Look carefully at your supporters. Epstein was a brilliant manipulator and, by surrounding himself with the trappings – mansion, airplane, swanky friends – he built a grandiose illusion of wealth and success. What sealed the deal, and what he promoted flagrantly, were the contributions he'd made to universities, hospitals, healthcare organizations, and the like. The idea that he was a big-shot philanthropist made everyone around him feel comfortable with whatever other improprieties they sensed. Or knew about.

We would later find out that multiple nonprofits he claimed to support showed no record of his donations. When asked to confirm or deny the purported gifts, many declined to comment. So why did these prominent institutions allow Epstein to issue press releases saying he donated money when he didn't? And why, when journalists asked whether they'd received the funds, did they decline to answer? Knowing what they likely knew about Epstein, why did they accept the money (or not) in the first place?

I think there are lots of reasons, but foremost among them is the belief that persists in fundraising that donors aren't regular people. That, no matter what, we must be handled with care.

So, we call the shots. Because you never know when we might donate again. And, let's face it, the rich tend to hang with the rich. If you're a donor and your friend is called out for bad (or, worst case, criminal) behavior, you might be considered guilty by association. You're likely going to freak out and you're very likely to curtail your giving.

I get it. Nonprofits can't sustain that sort of upheaval, especially when so many are held together by large annual gifts from a small group of donors. But I still want you to tell me the truth.

Emotional Baggage

Rebecca Stone is the 'unicorn' this discussion needs, a veteran fundraiser who works privately as a psychotherapist. Because of Rebecca's experience in both fields, she's in a great position to speak to some of the emotional issues at play in fundraising, and also offer advice on how to address them.

When Rebecca left the charitable sector, it was because she found 'the culture in many organizations, as well as the professional development opportunities, to be boring and banal,' despite what she calls the 'sacred task' that's at the center of fundraising. Still, Rebecca would eventually return to the world of nonprofits, and what she discovered was striking. As a therapist who specialized in the Hakomi Method (which uses a mindfulness-centered, somatic approach), she was a much better fundraiser.

Intrigued, Rebecca connected with friend and fellow Hakomi therapist Ariana Tosatto, who had a similar history in fundraising and sales. What would it be like, the women wondered, to design emotional intelligence training for fundraisers?

Hillel International held the inaugural workshop by Tosatto and Stone, and kudos to that organization for doing so. Called 'The Elephant in the Room,' the session focused on the psychology of money in the context of an 'ask,' with transformative results. Hillel has since hired the pair (along with The Fundraising School at the Indiana University Lilly Family School of Philanthropy) to create intensive training workshops that build fundraisers' skills in emotional intelligence. The training has participants learn about active listening; how to engage donors, rather than just pitch them, in deep conversations about values; and how to dive into their own emotional baggage about having money and asking for it. The Lilly School focuses more on the technical in this training, and Tosatto and Stone handle skill-building in emotional intelligence.

Rebecca bases some of what she does on the work of the Klontz doctors, renowned pioneers in financial psychology, who write about the different archetypes at play in our disordered relationships with money, and whose 'Money Disorder Assessment' is widely used by financial planners and psychologists. In relating the Klontz archetypes to fundraising, Rebecca explains, 'If I have *money worship* [an obsession with money on the one hand, and a feeling on the other that there will never be enough], I might get confrontational with my ask.'

'But if I have *money avoidance*,' she continues, 'I'm less likely to ask upfront. I might even dislike the donor in question because I bring an attitude to the conversation, in that I think money is stupid.

'Then, if I have *money relational conflict*, I might express it as a dislike of the power dynamic inherent in money. In this case, I might even feel that those with money have power over me to the extent that I'm guarded, or I otherwise impact the relationship because I don't trust that the person with money will treat me well.'

It's easy to see why there's traction here, among donors and fundraisers. All the more for the fact that, in her work with nonprofits, Rebecca adds to this emotional piece (with its focus on mindfulness techniques and active listening) business-type training and coaching.

For my part, I've always believed that if fundraisers can learn to really listen to donors – and, in the process, discover the link between their giving and their values – we'll be that much closer to authentic engagement. As Rebecca says, 'It's about getting people to go deeper, so that their relationships with donors are not about transaction and manipulation.'

ACHIEVABLE GOALS MAKE FOR BETTER RELATIONS

Rebecca Stone has identified at least one relatively easy way for sector leaders to implement change: realistic goal setting. Effective and humane, this practice shows leadership by not excluding those on the ground.

In my view, here's what usually happens:

- Targets aren't set by the fundraisers; sometimes, they're not even in the room.
- New fundraisers to the organization don't get any leeway. They're learning about mission and building relationships while also remaining accountable to goals.
- The goals are unrealistic, causing fundraiser anxiety, desperation, and burnout.
- Donors sense the desperation and are disinclined to help.
- If willing to stick it out, donors insist on dealing exclusively with very senior staff.
- The unrealistic goals aren't met, comprising the credibility of the organization with all involved.
- Fundraisers leave, and the feeling on both sides is that any relationships were just transactional.

Here's what to do instead:

- Ensure that fundraisers are in the room when establishing targets.
- Take their feedback as to what's realistic.
- Invite them to own the planning process, and likewise the goals.
- Consider adjusting the targets for new fundraisers to allow them time to develop relationships.
- Consider also adjusting their timelines.
- Share your relationship-based reasons for doing so.
- Acknowledge that deepening relationships with donors will rarely pay off in year one.

Donors Have Work to Do, Too

The truth is, donors have less to lose if their relationships with charities (or fundraisers) go south. The stakes just aren't as high for them. But stakes do exist, both personally and within the larger context of philanthropy. Here, as well, self-awareness is key.

Let's say that a fundraiser is doing me the great respect of helping me realize my philanthropic ambitions, just as Timothy Seiler from the Lilly Family School of Philanthropy suggested. I better be willing to acknowledge that respect and respond in kind.

As my donor friend Teri likes to say, 'it cuts both ways.' Teri believes donors need to be a lot more sensitive to the needs of the organizations they support. 'I think there are as many ways of giving,' she insists, 'as there are givers. Part of a donor's work is sorting that out on a personal level. So, it's *how* do you want to give, *where* do you want to give ... and then it's also what you want from relationships.'

CONSIDER PLAYING THE ROLE OF THE DONOR

Fundraisers: let's do a bit of role-playing. The premise is that you're a prospective donor who's agreed to a meeting. In this scenario, you've heard about the organization through a friend, so you first need to do some research. Research will make sure that you optimize your time and it might also let you bypass the spin – the pre-packaged 'sell' that tends to make you uncomfortable. How do you approach this process and make the most of the meeting itself?

Here are a few ideas:

- Check out the members of the organization's board; ditto for its staff.
- Find out how long it's been around.
- Figure out who will be at the meeting.

- Do a basic search of related websites and news articles.
- Skip Charity Navigator (see page 183) or else take the information it yields with a grain of salt.
- Treat any red flags raised by board members with the seriousness they deserve and cancel if that feels right – or conduct the meeting over coffee instead of lunch.

Then at the meeting, you ask questions:

- Can you tell me in your own words what your organization does?
- Why are you involved?
- What makes you passionate about it?
- What other organizations are doing something similar?
- How is what you do different?
- Does your organization have partners and, if so, who are they?
- Do you think your organization 'plays well' (in the collaborative sense) with others?
- Has it changed much since its inception?
- Where do you see it going in five years?
- What do you think stands in the way of that goal?
- Are there structural challenges? If so, what are they?
- If resources weren't an issue, how would you accomplish your goal?
- Besides money, what else does your organization need?
- How do you engage volunteers?
- How do you keep them?

- What do you most need out of a volunteer that you're not getting at the moment?

Finally, you ensure that you're honest yourself. For example:

- Here are my interests ... is there a fit here with what your organization is doing?
- Here's what I need to know ... and it doesn't require reports or handholding.
- Here's what you need to know ... I dislike galas, I prefer phone calls over lunch, I like to donate digitally, etc.
- I like to participate in some way with the organizations I support ... how would you deal with that?
- While I really appreciate the meeting, I'm not going to support your organization, and I don't want you to waste any more of your time ... is that something you can respect?
- Or, let's make a deal ... if you're going to ask me for money in future, can we agree that you'll tell me at the beginning of the conversation?

Relationships are just as important to many of the younger donors I spoke with. The difference is in their priorities. Often a primary concern is the beneficiary, and what level of respect exists between the organization doing the funding and the people it funds. This is part of social justice. For example,

Resource Generation chapter leader Andrea Pien has spoken to me of how the traditional power balance favors the donor. She says, 'There's so much fear and uncertainty on the side of the grantee. I see my job as evening the field.'

Typically, the organizations that Andrea and her peers support (we'll take a look at a couple of them in Chapter Six) are small and scrappy. But Andrea is considerate of their lack of capacity and, like many of us, values what's 'real': 'Because power usually starts with me, I try to lead with trust. I get a good feeling when people are honest in their answers to my questions, honest when they can't answer a question, and honest about where they need support.'

THE CLASS PRIVILEGE TEST

Whether you fund, fundraise or are funded, it's worth noting that Resource Generation (whose members we've already met) has a class privilege quiz. With a series of 'clues,' such as *Your parents, grandparents or other relatives paid for your education* and *Your passport has a lot of stamps on it* and *You chose to work a low-paying job* and *You eat a lot of organic food*, quiz-takers are invited to mindfully take stock of wealth inequality before signing the organization's Giving Pledge.

You can check it out here: https://resourcegeneration. org/start-your-journey/quiz/

Inspiring, right? Which, again, makes me question some of the advice that's circulating among nonprofits today about how to connect with Millennial donors, a topic I'll return to many times in the chapters to come. Sure, some of what's circulating is spot-on and productive. But there are also plenty of suggestions out there that are really demeaning. Such as:

- Make sure your pitch lasts twenty minutes or less. Millennials have short attention spans.
- Use the word 'technology' a lot. They like that.
- Use Facebook to connect with Millennials. They all use Facebook.
- Invite them to lunch. They're sure to enjoy a fancy lunch.
- Suggest a meeting or event in a bar. Millennials like bars – especially trendy ones.

While these examples speak for themselves, what they don't do is speak for Millennials. And that's a shame, since Millennials now represent our largest demographic, age-wise, and an equally large opportunity.

We really can't afford to screw it up.

What Happens When Charities Guess

If I were to make a Venn diagram specifically for fundraisers, I'd highlight the intersection of two sets in particular: organizational mission and donor interests. Where the two align is a sweet spot – this much, most of us know. It's finding it that can be tricky.

Back when I was managing the nascent web presence of a major studio, I was asked if the Internet could be used as an adjunct to traditional consumer research. Out of that query came one of the first online focus groups. Not only was it a huge success, it was also pretty simple stuff. From the comfort of our conference room, we interacted digitally with our target audience worldwide – fans, in this case, of two shows produced by the studio. Then we used their input to make decisions.

Decades have passed (and so much has changed) since my initial foray into online consumer research. Still, I was reminded of it recently when I came across a widely circulated 2019 survey from email marketing company Campaign Monitor. In it, nearly 59% of nonprofits insisted that live events were critical for attracting new donors, but just 18% of donors claimed to have learned about a charity through a live event. And if that weren't enough, nearly 50% of nonprofits said they believed donors preferred to connect with them through such events, but just 16% of donors chose events as a preferred method.

Distressing? It gets worse. A colleague of mine who specializes in nonprofit communications put the reason for the disconnect down to guesswork. His theory was not that nonprofits were acting on bad data – because more often than not, he felt, they didn't *have* any data. But they did have a mandate to attract new donors, so they made a guess about best practices based largely on their own preferences. Which, as we now know, had almost nothing to do with *donor* preferences, so they were therefore doomed to fail.

Is it indulgent to suggest that we solicit feedback from donors? People often think so, as if in identifying what they want we're going to abandon organizational mission – or at least modify it to the extent that it sells. This just flat out isn't true.

The right research can actually strengthen mission. It gives us insight into how best to communicate – probably not at an event, for example – what it is that we do. Even better, it helps us identify the donors who are most likely to share that vision. It puts us in the sweet spot.

Knowing this, I have to wonder why so many nonprofits either: a) do what they like and ignore donor insights, if they collect them at all; or b) do what they *assume* donors like, compromising mission and strategy in favor of the sort of 'wink-wink' pandering that's about as convincing as a kid in a class play.

It happens all the time. Just recently, a local nonprofit asked me to be part of a conversation about approaching new donors. The meeting started well, and there was lots of enthusiasm, but the ideas put forth (think snail mail and the telephone) were arcane, and not at all in line with what I've observed about donor behavior. Then we shifted focus, abandoning the agenda altogether to talk instead about donor *value*, and limiting our targets to those *with money*.

Before the new slogan or mailing or pitch, even before the search for new prospects, why not reach out to a group of donors and ask them what they're about? Find out how they like to learn about charities, and what sort of appetite they have for metrics or story. If they've experienced a pitch that didn't go so well, ask them why. Likewise, if the pitch was successful.

And so on.

This sort of information is critical to business success, just as it is to success in fundraising. The difference is that, in fundraising (at least historically), we don't do enough digging.

But here's the thing, if you've ever wondered whether research can both service mission and help build new relationships, while *also* stemming the tide of donor attrition – the answer is yes. You bet it can.

The Five-Minute Google Search

Let's say we have yet to meet, but I *am* on your radar. Maybe we've set up a call? Wouldn't it be great if there were a place you could go for information, somewhere quick, easy, and free?

I can't promote this one enough. You've heard me complain about being asked – usually over lunch with fundraisers, for which I've sacrificed time with my kids – what my husband does or whether I've ever had a career or enjoy the arts. The lack of preparation astounds me.

Now consider this. Not so long ago, the director of development for an LA charity arrived for a meeting at the house. Her work had something to do with animal welfare; that much I'd learned over email. But we hadn't met. Introductions were exchanged over coffee in our kitchen, and then in walked the family dog.

The woman said, 'That's Lucy. She's a Pitbull mix. She's also a rescue.'

I looked at her, amazed. 'How do you know that?'

She knew it from a Google search.

THE FIVE-MINUTE GOOGLE SEARCH

In fundraising, most donor searches start and end with publicly available financial information: political affiliation, recorded political donations, and the value of the donor's house.

Here's why this is irrelevant:

- Political affiliation is a non-starter, since prospective donors usually have a connection to the organization already – that's why they're on the prospects' list.
- Political donations have zero to tell us about a prospective donor's capacity because they're capped.
- The value of a donor's home is likewise not helpful. Who knows how that home has been leveraged?

Here's what to do instead:

- Google the donor's name and see which organizations pop up. These will tell you a great deal about the person's interests.
- Follow your Google results to LinkedIn, where you can see the donor's work history. Consider making a personal connection over shared skills or contacts.
- Scan the search yield for news articles or blog posts written about or by your donor. These will give you added insight into the person's outlook and priorities.

Then, if your initial connection to the donor was through a mutual friend or colleague, ask that person for any other details that might prove useful (such as donor likes and dislikes, preferences for communication, level of comfort with formality, habitual ways of working, and so on).

Sound too easy? Take a look at what you can learn about yourself in a Five-Minute Google Search. You might be surprised.

The Elevator Approach
to Opportunity

We're now knee-deep into the process of stacking the odds in our favor, at least as far as relationships go. Next, we'll look at the 'ask', and how donors and funders can talk about money. It's a critical chapter.

Before we get there, here's one last story.

I found myself running late recently for a charity event in San Francisco. Although the hotel room I had booked was just upstairs, I still managed to leave it in a panic. I turned to the mirror in the elevator as soon as the doors closed behind me, really just to check my hair. 'Oh,' said the other passenger, a young woman whom I'd barely registered, 'can I help you with that?'

That's odd, I thought – until I saw her cart. It overflowed with all sorts of hairdressing tools and products because, as it turns out, she'd just left a client. 'Here,' she said, professional comb already in hand, 'let me fix your hair.' Once the doors opened into the lobby, she sprayed it too, and then we both went off in different directions.

Not before I'd asked for her card, however, and promised I'd be in touch on my next visit to the city.

The 'elevator pitch,' whether it occurs literally or not, is nothing new. Still, this brief and to-the-point yet somehow meaningful interaction (which actually played out between floors in an elevator) makes me marvel at its implicit lesson.

And maybe because of where I was headed that evening, it also makes me think of nonprofits.

For profits, particularly start-ups looking for funding, tend to have staff that are incredibly skilled on their feet. Once they see potential in the form of a future customer or funding source, they can't unsee it. They'll work to make the most of just about any interaction. And because they've also worked on their 'elevator pitch,' it's good. Really good. Clear, concise and compelling, it's that elusive triple threat.

Nonprofits are another story. Those associated with charitable organizations often tank when, at a moment's notice, they try to describe what their organizations do. And yet we all have a stake in the game, whether we're members of the board, the executive, senior management or junior staff. Which means that we all need to practice those elevator speeches with the people or projects in mind whose existence depends on them.

Of course, as a volunteer I'm responsible too. I can't tell you the number of times I've asked someone in passing what they do for a living, and their response went something like this: 'Oh, I work for a nonprofit.' Or, 'I sit on a few boards.'

For some reason, it's up to me to press them for details. 'What sort of nonprofit?'

'We do work in Africa.'

'What sort of work?'

'We build schools for girls.'

That, right there, is elevator material. Don't ever leave home without it.

FOUR

MONEY TALKS

*Authentic Ways to Deal
with the 'Ask'*

My friend Noa and I are biding our time, catching up before the start of another 'rubber chicken' dinner. Even in a ball-room, Noa's intense. 'Lisa,' she says, eyeing a cluster of fund-raisers, 'I will not serve you up to the world.'

Noa's comment was a little jarring, but I knew what she meant. Noa holds a senior position at a nonprofit research institution, and she's also very dear to me. When one of the board members of Noa's institution discovered that she was my friend, this board member insisted she step away from the relationship. 'You can't be Lisa's friend,' he said, 'because Lisa has capacity.'

The message from Noa's nonprofit? What's *personal* (for example, friendship) and what *pays* (potentially, me) cannot coexist. Money comes first.

Another friend of mine, Sara, stays with us at our house when she's in LA. Sara works for an organization whose leaders I know, an organization we also support, from time to time.

But when these leaders got wind of Sara's visits, they were full of questions. About me, my family, our habits. Then they let Sara know that, if she's staying at our home, it's not only her obligation to remain in the friendship, but also to *use* it by asking me for *more* money.

The message from Sara's nonprofit? Forget the personal, even if you find yourself in your pjs in Lisa's kitchen, drinking coffee, and discussing your kids. As a donor, Lisa's just a dollar sign. Money comes first.

Obviously, money is essential to philanthropy. But what these two nonprofits assume is that money and authenticity are at odds. When push comes to shove, according to each of them, a fundraiser must choose money. This is counterproductive. Take Noa and Sara. Although they both work in the philanthropic sector, they share the conviction that authenticity is more important than money. The fact that they believe this makes money easier to procure. Noa and Sara are true to their respective causes while keeping true to themselves, and donors see and respond to their sincerity.

Many donors will also have to make a choice about being true to themselves and their values at some point or another in their philanthropic journeys. I've had plenty of moments myself where I felt compelled to donate to organizations, despite being somewhat uncomfortable. In cases, for example, of a quid pro quo, I knew the source of my discomfort. But sometimes I didn't know, and that's when I did some digging. I uncovered extremism in different forms – religious, political – which, at the end of the day, forced me to define my personal red lines.

There is no recipe for success in every situation, because those red lines are as variable as donors are, sometimes even changing over time. Researching your prospects can help with that, as we discussed in the last chapter. So too does the knowledge that, as donors and fundraisers, we practice philanthropy because we care.

And *because* we care, having those authentic conversations, even if they involve an 'ask' for money, can and should be a whole lot easier.

WHY I BROKE UP WITH MY DAF

What does authenticity have to do with Donor Advised Funds?

Let me explain:

Obviously, if I'm authentic, I'm 'true.' I want my interactions with others to be 'true' as well, because that's how I show integrity. The problem is that, once you add money to the mix, or a charitable transaction, being true (or even just being open) becomes a whole lot harder. It's still important, though, which is why 'transparency' is such a buzzword in business and governance.

I first wrote about my DAF in Chapter Two and you'll remember my point about a percentage of its administrative fees going back to the organization that houses it. I knew when I started thinking about DAFs that I wanted mine to benefit the Jewish community and progressive causes, so I opened one at the Jewish Community Foundation of Los Angeles (JCFLA). I even joined the Foundation's board. What I didn't know – and what wasn't transparent, at least to me – was that in housing my DAF where I did, I could no longer give to just anybody.

You're probably already aware that many Jewish community members disagree on the issue of what's good for Israel. Even so, we should all be able to agree that, as individuals, we have the right to make our own choices about how we support this community. Doesn't that go without saying, especially where money is concerned?

Not necessarily. I learned this the hard way when I tried to donate through my DAF to IfNotNow, a progressive organization that's working to move the needle in our collective conversations about Israel. Basically, the JCFLA (which is the planned giving arm of the Jewish Federation of Greater Los Angeles) blocked my donation. And that's when I discovered that, while I *can* choose where my DAF money goes, the organization housing that DAF retains right of refusal. Meaning, the organization approves the grant and not the donor. The donor gives up that right when she opens her DAF.

It's a lot to take in. When I asked the JCFLA why it was drawing the line at IfNotNow, I was told that it had every right to do so. I then asked for a policy statement and received a set of funding guidelines, which were extremely vague. The truth is, IfNotNow had a different set of values, some of which it expressed by protesting Jewish establishment groups, and that's why the JCFLA didn't want to support it. But as far as I could tell, the JCFLA had drawn no such line on the right.

Ultimately, I transferred my money out of that DAF and into one more aligned with *my* values. My experience was also featured in the Jewish press, which made me realize that other donors out there had similar concerns. Still, nobody I shared my story with personally had heard of a DAF donation being blocked for any other reason than that the charity on the receiving end of the donation failed to classify, under US tax law, as a tax-exempt nonprofit organization, or 501(c)(3).

As is the case in other philanthropic spaces, the trend we're seeing with DAFs has donors asking more questions – in this case, of organizations such as the JCFLA – in their desire for transparency. It's only natural for donors to want to feel good about what their charitable giving programs fund, so the fact that they're taking matters into their own hands and pushing back against ambiguities in policy is a really good thing. It's also another sign (fundraisers, take note!) that the money conversation is still a *values* conversation. That's why it's so important to be authentic.

You Can't Fake the Hustle

First impressions are the strongest. That's why this chapter puts donors and fundraisers together, usually in 'first-date' scenarios, to take a look at the 'ask' for money. Much of what we cover here will be revisited in later chapters. In the meantime, I suspect you'll all agree that asking for money (or working hard for money, which is really what I mean by the 'hustle') is about as real as things get in philanthropy. It's what brings in the cash to build that shelter for the homeless, clean up our oceans, or send Afghan girls to school.

Here's the thing, though. Unlike what Noa and Sara were told, foregoing the personal to put money first is never a good idea. Donors are human. If an interaction is staged or if it's super uncomfortable – as Sara's would have been, had she asked for money in her pjs in my kitchen – I can tell. Just as I can tell when you're trying to be polite, driveling on about my pretty hair color when you're really just after my money.

Faking it, forcing it, being coy about it, or being impersonal – none of it promotes success. And nor does it set us up for anything resembling an actual relationship.

Ours is a sector with heart. Philanthropy has its systems, however, and these make authentic relationships hard. If you're a fundraiser, you've got a book of contacts you need to go through; you've got quarterly targets – where do you find the time to develop relationships? Getting excited about an organization is probably also a challenge given how likely you are to leave it behind. (As you'll remember from page 36, the research shows that fundraisers typically spend just sixteen to eighteen months at any given organization.)

Do these systems make it impossible to connect? They do make it difficult. But if, together, we work toward being more upfront in our communications about money, if we stop tiptoeing around it, and, miracle of miracles, *talk* – well, we might just have a chance at something real.

The Carpet-Bombing Approach to Donor Solicitation

This is where we get to the irony. While it's 'impolite' to speak frankly with donors about money in *certain* circumstances, it's somehow okay to flat-out harass them about money in others. I'm referring here to the carpet-bombing approach to donor solicitation, an unconscionable sector favorite.

Back in the days when the rules for fundraising were created, someone must have decided that calling a prospective donor over and over again would result in success. I have to wonder if any evidence exists to support this approach, because it sure is annoying. So much so, in my case, that the organization responsible for the calls will suffer a hit to its credibility in my eyes, and therefore the trust I'm willing to afford it in the future. At a given point, I'm so turned off that I can't imagine *ever* supporting it.

This doesn't happen after the second call, or even the third. I'm talking about a *lot* of calls. Which is so common in my world that I found myself reacting strongly to a recent article on the topic in the *Chronicle of Philanthropy*. Called 'The Future of College Phone-athons,' the article uses the words 'innovative' and 'counterintuitive' to describe an overhaul to the practice carried out in 2016 at Colorado State University (CSU).

CSU decided to stop contacting people who hadn't answered a phone-athon call in ten years of regular calling. I nearly fell out of my chair. Ten years?! Even the university's own Meg Weber, whose position at the time was Executive Director of Annual Giving, was seemingly at a loss. 'If someone asks you out on a date for ten years straight,' Meg is quoted as saying, 'and you keep saying no or ignoring them, at some point it becomes stalking, right?'

It turns out that 70,000 people received calls from CSU – regular calls, over a ten-year period – without ever once answering the phone. Forgive me, CSU, but I have to assume that the calls were happening for longer than the ten years stipulated; fundraisers probably established a number (of years of calling) that simply felt suitably long. And I have to think, too, of the associated costs. How much money could possibly have been raised relative to the expense incurred over those years by staffing, database maintenance, and so on? Then there's the fact that, prior to its phone-athon overhaul, CSU alumni who 'gave frequently but never by phone' were *also* being called. What?!

There are so many issues here that we'll unpack in Chapter Seven, with its focus on communications. It's enough to say for now that what should have occurred, years ago, is some vital surgery to those CSU call lists. Many nonprofits do a good job these days of parsing their lists. And well they should, since, with technology at our disposal, it's never been easier. Just as many (if not more) nonprofits, however, exercise little discipline in this regard, and the consequences are killing them.

So, telephone junkies beware. If it takes a decade for you to accept that I'm just not your guy, there is a problem. There is likewise a problem if you've got me on your call list when your records show clearly that I give by other means. If you carpet-bomb me with requests for $100 when I give to you annually at a much higher level – well, I don't even have the words.

EMERGENCY ASKS AND THE BOY WHO CRIED WOLF

First, a caveat: this is not about actual emergencies.

Still, you know the drill. A last-minute demand is issued to prospective donors, instead of a thoughtful 'ask.' Email is popular, in terms of communicating this demand, as are exclamation marks. Often the subject lines look something like this: 'LAST CHANCE TO GIVE!' Or, 'BEFORE IT'S TOO LATE!'

Sometimes these emails make donors responsible: 'WE'RE SHORT ON OUR GOAL! SEND MONEY!' And sometimes they deliver a threat: 'KIDS WILL QUIT SCHOOL IF YOU DON'T HELP TODAY!'

Read *one* of these emails and you might feel compassion. Read 200 of them in a day, as I have (see page 231) during the peak fundraising 'push' of Giving Tuesday and December 31, and you might start to feel like your house is on fire.

Not good. Also, not good for giving.

Rosso Fellow Timothy Seiler from the Lilly Family School of Philanthropy has spoken to me about what he calls 'the scolding model' of fundraising. The scolding model playbook goes something like this: 'We need X amount of money as a charity, so you need to give it to us … and you need to give it to us right away.' The model does work for some, Timothy says, and it's certainly proven effective for Giving Tuesday. But for every person for whom it works, there are probably legions of others who find it offensive.

So, parse your lists. Stop being melodramatic in your communications, and instead be straightforward. Finally, try not to conflate what *you* need as a charity with what your donors need. We're smart enough to know the difference.

As the Scouts Say, Be Prepared

Let's say you're a fundraiser who believes passionately in the wonderful work of your organization. That's fabulous, but it's only a start. If you can't communicate – in a language I understand – *why* the work is wonderful, your pitch is going to fail.

And if your pitch goes south because you haven't prepared, failure is the least of your worries. An ill-prepared pitch can be downright offensive to donors. It suggests that you don't care quite enough to come informed – be it about us (your prospective donors) or your cause – and that means you're wasting our time.

If you've stolen two hours that I'll never get back, you're unlikely to get *me* back. Ever. This makes me sad for both of us.

Long before we met – and for more years than we care to admit – Josh was a Boy Scout and I was a Girl Scout. We both went on to careers in business. In the decades that followed, we each came to realize that the Scouts motto, which is 'be prepared,' was just as essential in our careers as it had been in our youth.

In business, success is about finding the place where preparation and opportunity meet. The same is true in fundraising.

I'm going to assume that you've taken to heart some of the stories I told in Chapter Three, about the value of research. Add to that effective list parsing (as we explored in relation to phone-athons) and you're halfway there – at least with respect to your prospects. You can bring these prospects to life by creating giving profiles: a *who, why, what, how,* and *where* for every one of them. But do remember this: it's never good to prioritize prospects based only on their capacity to give.

What you *can* do, as part of your 'Scouts' approach, is scan the horizon regularly in order to add to your people-with-capacity list. The methods we just explored are only the beginning. Search tools exist in business, for example, that are completely ignored by fundraisers – with one of the best, EDGAR Online, discussed right here. The important thing to remember is that the exercise of looking for new donors puts you in that place where preparation and opportunity meet.

EDGAR ONLINE

We have already explored (see pages 107–8) the small miracle of the 'Five-Minute Google Search', and what it can tell nonprofits about prospective donors. EDGAR Online is another search mechanism that, to my continued amazement, charities overlook – so much so that I have yet to encounter a single fundraiser who has put it to use.

EDGAR stands for 'electronic data gathering, analysis and retrieval.' EDGAR Online takes its name from the EDGAR database of the United States Securities and Exchange Commission, which makes available public financial data for all public companies, including those about to file. It's basically an online intelligence tool for global investors, for whom it creates and distributes data and public filings for equities, mutual funds and other publicly traded assets.

Why did it take a single day for stockbrokers and real estate agents to find us after the IPO, when it took charities well over a year? EDGAR Online is why.

It's really that simple. Add this bit of prep to your arsenal and you'll get a wealth of insight into future donors. Most of the data you'll access via EDGAR Online is available for download and some of it can be viewed for free. The platform also offers a subscription-based service for financial professionals (fundraisers, take note!) that enables subscribers to do things such as access advanced search features, customize and aggregate only the information they need, and receive alerts when tracked data changes.

As you move toward tailoring your pitch, another thing to consider is demographics. While it's dangerous to make assumptions based solely on something like age, it's also unwise to forget age altogether. Generational tendencies matter.

Ted, the Millennial son of a friend of mine, runs a nonprofit. He likes to use the Rotary Club as an example of a legacy approach to fundraising that's both behind the times and out of touch with its audiences. 'I've been asked to speak at a lot of Rotary luncheons,' Ted told me, 'and the format is, basically, that you describe what you're doing and then you say thanks. You're not allowed to ask for money, so people have to approach your privately if they want to offer support. And the chances of that happening are slim, in my opinion, because you're not supposed to deal with tangibles in your talk. You can't say, for example, "this is the amount we need, and this is what we'll do with it."

'I have no problem asking for money, and no problem when people say no. That's the healthy approach to fundraising. The Rotary will take your dues, which it tends to distribute to old-school charities, and it will promise you benefits. But young people like myself just aren't interested in spending Fridays eating lunch and listening to random speakers talk about causes that they can't really get behind. It's pointless.'

As a Millennial, Ted's disaffection with these old-school approaches is not uncommon. Still, had he known in advance about the 'rules' for Rotary Club luncheons, he might have been willing to deliver a marketing presentation instead of one that was focused on fundraising. He might have prepared differently, in that event, and/or adjusted his expectations.

It's also possible that, with a little more information, Ted might have said no altogether. (Remember, he described these luncheons as 'pointless.') Either way, Ted probably should have done more to 'know' the Rotary Club before he took to the mike. But the Rotary should *also* have known – and considered – the people it was bringing together.

Knowing what to expect (or, at the very least, anticipate) is just part of preparation. Donors of all ages appreciate it too. As you're about to read, *not* preparing a donor – or being obtuse about a meeting's purpose – could cost you dearly.

WHEN THE CASE FOR $1M WAS $25K

Josh and I used to give to a certain international relief organization. We became acquainted with the organization after attending a few of its events, and our friends were supporters. I loved the woman who was running it at the time, and I thought: this is perfect. We came forward with a gift of $25K. Substantial, in our minds.

The organization encouraged us to become more involved. We helped out here and there but kept fielding invitations to go on their trips. A lot of organizations, particularly those with an international focus, want you to go on their trips. Often, they're what I call 'study tours,' and they're sort of designed to get you to give more. That's fine, in my view, only we have kids and they've got school. We can't just leave.

The leaders of this nonprofit continued to ask, however. 'Won't you come? Won't you come?' Which started to make me feel like I wasn't a good donor.

Fast forward a year, and I was asked again for my annual gift. Not once had anybody clarified that my $25K was annual, but I was too shocked to say no. I kept giving.

Time passed and I was invited for an annual update. 'We'd love to see you,' the fundraisers said, setting up a meeting that turned out to be great. At least initially. I appreciated the information they provided on the status of their programs, and they in turn seemed to appreciate *me*.

That is, until they asked me flat-out for a million dollars. The message was that because I'd given a million dollars to other organizations, I should also be giving it to them.

Here's the thing. Nobody ever asked me where the organization sat on my list of priorities. Nobody ever said, for example, 'Where are we in relation to the other charities you support?' Or, 'Is ours a priority cause for you?' I'm pretty sure they didn't want to know.

And while I understand the desire to be first – number one among causes, or at least as important as the ones at the top – what I can't understand, to this day, is those fund-raisers. How could they let that happen? Their presumptuous behavior made me feel that my gifts had been meaningless; that my $25K was pennies to them and that as one of their supporters, I had let them down.

I did get an apology after the fact, but I no longer contribute to the organization. And that's sad. So, before you insist among yourselves that 'it doesn't hurt to ask,' please remember that sometimes, unfortunately, it does.

The Very Real Business of 'Asks'

I don't want to give to an organization that can afford to pay someone to sit with me through six meetings before ever getting to the business at hand. That's a pretend relationship, and it's nauseating. So much better is the dynamic I have with

New Israel Fund CEO Daniel Sokatch. Daniel says, 'Lisa, if our meeting involves an ask, I will tell you in advance.'

Then there's Big Sunday's David Levinson, whom I introduced in Chapter One. David told me about once coming across a book on fundraising. 'The book insisted that it was necessary to make "three touches" before every ask. I hate that shit. People are people; they're not money machines. I want donors to know that if we run into each other at a bar mitzvah or at the bagel store, I'm happy to see you because I like you. It's great to catch up, have a laugh, and schmooze. And in those situations, I'll be very sure – and very happy and relieved, actually – to not ask you for a dime.'

This isn't about *not* working hard for your cause; quite the opposite. Business is business, as they say, and schnapps is schnapps. Navigating fundraising's complex relationships is only going to work, at least in the long term, if we're straight with one another about the nature of our interactions.

For example, bringing the equivalent of a babysitter to our meeting is not a very 'straight' way to start. These babysitters are usually people I know, often just peripherally. Fundraisers will bring one of them to a pitch in order to enhance their ability to get money out of me. I guess the idea is that I'll feel more comfortable with the situation if I recognize a friendly face. In reality, though, it feels like a playdate. And worse than a playdate, because it's forced.

PITCHING EMERGING DONORS

What I hear	What I want to hear
We'd like to take you and your husband to lunch.	We'd love to tell you about our organization. What's convenient for you?
We help sick children. You should help us in our mission to give these kids some hope.	What are your giving priorities? Might there be a fit between what we do and your giving goals?
Here's a glossy brochure that outlines our programs.	I'd love to discuss our mission with you, and also show you how we help and why we're different. I'm here to answer any (and all!) of your questions.
We're asking for a gift of $25K.	What would you consider a meaningful gift?
For a donation of a certain size, we'll invite you to sit on the board of trustees.	How would you like to be involved with this organization? Do you have any skills you can contribute? Are you interested in being engaged in a hands-on way by volunteering with our families? Or would you prefer not to be involved over and above your actual gift?

If you're not interested in a donation of that size, perhaps something smaller?	I see we're not a great fit for you. Can you connect us with any friends who might be a better fit?
We'd appreciate a donation of any size.	I see we're not a great fit for you. I'm sorry about that. Would it be okay for me to continue to send you occasional emails if I think there is something in them that aligns with your interests?
So, you don't want to give us anything?	I see we're not a great fit for you. I don't know whether you've heard of [insert name of organization]. It does great work and might be better in line with your giving goals. I'm happy to make an introduction.

Again, I come from business. Not only am I used to being pitched, I've pitched myself. Which is why I'm a proponent, as you're about to read, of the Shark Tank approach. This has been popularized on television, and I suspect it got its name from all the entrepreneurs out there whose desire to 'live' (and be rewarded by the shark-like investors) is about as intense as their fear of elimination (by way of their ideas being condemned by said investors).

I was working in Hollywood when Silicon Valley became a Mecca for tech. People kept coming to the studios because they all wanted to say that their technology had been purchased by Universal or was part of the next big thing at NBC. They'd do these presentations that made no sense (for example, 'IP' to them was Internet Protocol, whereas to us it was Intellectual Property. Nobody translated!).

When I left the industry and started consulting, I went back to these guys and said, 'Look, I can get you the meetings you want. But unless you do the work – unless you're prepared to speak the language – I'm unwilling to schedule them.

'It's the difference,' I told them, 'between IP and IP.'

ADOPTING A SHARK TANK APPROACH TO FIRST MEETINGS

To ace any introductory meeting, be ready with the following:

- Enough knowledge about me to have an informed conversation
- An elevator pitch you know well enough to customize, depending on conversation flow
- An ability to talk about the need informing your organization's mission
- A compelling story to tell about its programs
- A few metrics that illustrate your organization's success (or point to it, if you're new)
- Details about how you are like or unlike related organizations

- Examples of how you 'play well with others' (or collaborate with like-minded organizations)
- A solid, structured ask, but enough flexibility to go off-book
- The foresight to know that 'acing' a meeting doesn't always mean the donor says *yes*

If questions come up in the meeting that stump you, don't make stuff up. Instead say:

- 'These are great questions. I'll do some research and get back to you.'
- 'I can't answer that, but I *will* connect you with our program director. She's happy to talk.'
- 'I haven't heard of the organization you mentioned. Can you tell me about it?'
- 'I'm not sure what they do, but here's what *we* do. Do you know how we're different?'
- 'Collaborating with them is an interesting idea. What do you envision?'
- 'I don't think we do that. Can you explain why you think it's something we should consider?

The Shark Tank approach is not without its criticisms. Opponents to it insist that it pits charity against charity, creating competition at a time when the pickings are slim (and the pool of donors out there is limited). I disagree. There is more than enough money to go around, especially if we get good at accessing it. All the approach does is force us into a place where we should be anyway – a place of preparedness. Maybe you adopt it merely to ready yourself, before meeting alone with one of your prospects. Or maybe you use it to compete at an event, as we'll discuss in Chapter Eight. The point is to *use* it.

In doing so, you'll clarify your strategy with the 'ask,' and also discover where you're flexible. You'll consider your audience, even if it's an audience of one. Finally, you'll advocate for what you believe in. That's the best part, and it works.

RECONSIDERING MULTI-YEAR GIFTS

Who doesn't want a gift that keeps on giving?

Annual or multi-year gifts represent ongoing support. With this support, development professionals get to relax a little, and maybe even spend more time on strategy. Annual or multi-year gifts also help ensure an organization's business objectives are a realistic expression of that strategy, something that's so much easier when you know what's coming in. And, they free up resources, because any fundraisers in the organization who might have had to work to renew or increase one-time donations can now spend their time finding *new* supporters.

Committing to give annually or over a specific number of years lets donors relax too. Lose the stress of the constant 'ask' and you gain a shot at broadening your relationship with the organization you support. Obviously, this benefits everyone.

Multi-year gifts and recurring donations are the holy grail of fundraising. They're among the best that the sector has to offer. What I'd like to see in the way of improvements is a little more flexibility in how these gifts are structured, and a lot more foresight in how they're tracked and reported. Here are a couple of ways we can get there:

- Why not value a multi-year gift that is equal in dollar amount to a one-time gift, well, *equally*? I get that there are reporting issues, of course. I also get that the multi-year thing means you can't ask for more money next year. But come on. Maybe you can't log that million today, but your organization still benefits (see above) as does our relationship.

- If you're willing to commit to #1, how about communicating a suite of options in your conversations with prospective donors? For example, you might discuss the virtues of a gift that's recurring, and what it can mean to give (and get!) the same amount annually. Or maybe what's attractive to your prospect is the idea of a major gift, such as $1M, that's split into increments given over a five-year period.

Ultimately, it's about playing the long game *and* stretching the win, and the sustainability of the sector depends on it.

When There Are Bills to Pay

Development professionals raise millions for the organizations they support. Collectively, they raise billions. Yet, according to a 2019 article published in *The Chronicle of Philanthropy*, just 31% of them feel comfortable talking with grant-makers about the need for general operating support.

Flip that statistic and you get a whopping 69%. These are the fundraisers who don't feel comfortable discussing the issue, and their prevalence in the sector makes me wonder how organizations manage to raise enough money to cover the costs of staffing, administration, and overhead. Then, too, I worry that *we* are to blame. The donors. That we must have made it clear, at some point, that we won't fork over for operational expenses.

If I were to attribute that statistic to a fictional cast of fundraisers, this is how it might look:

1. Katie, our first fundraiser, got shut down by one or more donors when she asked for a donation that included overhead. Now Katie is shell-shocked.
2. Marty, our second fundraiser, is embarrassed to seek funding for ops. Because the funding would cover his salary, he's not comfortable discussing it. Marty wants donors to believe that he cares enough to work for free.
3. Jala, our third fundraiser, was taught *never* to mention overhead. If you do, Jala was warned, donors will feel

forced to assess your percentages – money for ops against money for cause. Your pitch will be ruined.

4. Deb, our fourth fundraiser, just isn't into numbers. Deb is super skilled and knowledgeable, but operating budgets confuse her. She doesn't want to look dumb, so she avoids the topic completely.

5. Miguel, our fifth fundraiser, is a romantic. He loves to pitch, loves the cause, and wants only to focus on impact. Budgets aren't just boring for Miguel; they're vulgar. Miguel is in the game to change the world.

Not so fictional, is it? All you have to do now is factor into this mix some of the money disorders we discussed in Chapter Three and you can see how challenging it is to ask for unrestricted support or support for operations. But if you pitch a donor and skirt the issue of overhead, or avoid it altogether, you jeopardize your 'ask.' Donors are smart and they're also experienced. If they're anything like me, they'll sense your avoidance. Trust takes a hit and, with it, the credibility of your organization. That's a hard thing to get over.

The good news is that opportunity awaits. If fundraisers are willing to be honest, even matter-of-fact about what it costs to raise money, they'll likely convey professionalism to donors, as well as the sense, where budgets are concerned, that their organizations are governed by the principles of business. As the old adage goes, it takes money to make money – or, in this case, to raise, distribute, and monitor it.

Let's say I'm having lunch with Marty. I get that he's uncomfortable discussing his salary. I also get that he *needs* a salary. Marty may believe that a 100%-to-cause donation holds more appeal, but I'm just as aware as he is that such donations are possible only when overhead is funded by other means. And I'm not alone. In recent years, donors have been trained to be aware of the costs of procuring donations. To give one example, most online giving apps now ask for a percentage amount to cover costs. The 2–5% that's standard on these apps typically only covers the credit card fee. I've seen requests for up to 15%, which still isn't enough to run a charity. But the message – that it costs money to raise money – is getting out there and being heard.

We'll explore accountability issues in Chapter Six, because they definitely exist. In the meantime, rest assured that donors like me will give to an organization that gets results – even if the organization scores high, relatively speaking, on operational and administrative spending. Much better this than a frugal charity that isn't run professionally or can't manage to make an impact with its cause.

Donor Advised Funds, Revisited

Here's a thought. DAFs are downright huge, as we already know. They're also under-utilized. What if it were possible to figure out how to get at those funds – not only to advance the great work of our charities, but also to cover our costs?

Should you need reminding, we're talking about well over $100 billion sitting in DAFs, as I write this.

FINALLY, A DEDICATED WIDGET FOR DAFS

I happened to make an amazing discovery recently while visiting the website of Pine Street Inn, an organization that's working to end homelessness. Not only does Pine Street Inn include 'Donor Advised Funds' as a menu item among its online giving options, it also posts a widget that enables donors to give via their DAFs with ease.

Called 'DAF Direct,' the widget lets anyone with a DAF recommend a grant immediately – the only condition being that the DAF's sponsoring organization must be a participant in the DAF Direct program. There are no download or transaction fees for nonprofit or donor, so the DAF Direct widget (or the DAF Direct link, which is also an option for charities) represents a viable means for nonprofits to grow their donor base. And, since most DAF donors do research on nonprofit and third-party websites prior to giving, according to Schwab Charitable, this bit of new technology really is a no-brainer.

Of the hundreds of solicitations I've received, each inviting me to sponsor a nonprofit or buy tickets to a charity event, only one has included prominent mention of DAFs as a method of payment. This exception to the rule was Sharsheret, a nonprofit that helps women with breast cancer. Josh and I hosted a fundraiser for Sharsheret in our home recently (we do a lot of hosting – see Chapter Eight) and I was thrilled to see the words 'Donor Advised Fund' on the event's invitation and payment card. 'Donor Advised Fund' was right there with the usual suspects ('Cash, Check or Credit Card') and I swear I wanted to stand up and cheer.

TWO RECENT CHANGES THAT INFLUENCE GIVING

Albert Einstein once said that the hardest thing to understand in the world is income tax. Most of us can relate, which is why it's important to be aware of the following:

New tax laws were introduced in the US in January 2019, and the jury's still out about their effect on the charity sector. Because the standard deduction amount for charitable contributions was raised, taxpayers might now choose to take the deduction rather than itemize. Additionally, certain donations are now eligible for partial credit only. There are all sorts of ways that funders *and* fundraisers can optimize these changes, but knowledge is key. You can find a primer on the tax reform here: www.irs.gov/newsroom/tax-reform-news.

Donor Advised Funds don't represent a recent change per se, but they're driving the matter of *when* people give, and that's a newish concern. Or at least it should be in the world of nonprofits. I'll talk in detail in Chapter Seven about the dangers of the end-of-year giving push that's so universally favored by charities. But do know for now that anyone with a DAF isn't required to give at the end of the calendar year to claim a tax deduction. Instead, those of us with DAFs give money to organizations as we fall in love with them, on our own time. The frenzy of the fourth quarter – which we're made aware of in the uptick each year in asks for money – is mostly irrelevant. Charities need to retire this relic of how things used to be done (or at the very least, identify donors with DAFs) and move on.

Fundraisers, I can't ask enough that you learn about DAFs. Afterward, share what you learn with everyone in your organization, including your board members. One thing you'll discover in the process is that, although DAFs have been around for nearly fifty years, they're also a whole new animal, as far as charities go. For example, identifying the 'owners' of a DAF (really, the 'advisors') is tricky. As is establishing the amount of money sitting in individual DAF accounts. Technically, the institution that houses the DAF owns the funds, and that institution has no obligation to disclose this information. Nor does it have to tell you who directs how those funds are spent.

Still, it isn't rocket science. It's really just opportunity. And that, as per one of the simpler definitions in the *Oxford Dictionary of English*, is 'a set of circumstance that make it possible to do something.'

You didn't come to this book – and I didn't write it – for anything less.

HOW FUNDRAISERS CAN TAP INTO DAFS

- You already keep data on your donors. Ask every one of them if they have a DAF and then add that information to your files. Doing this will provide insight into their motivations for giving and also hint at whether or not they're likely to give at the end of the calendar year for tax reasons.
- Include the option to pay via DAF in any solicitation that includes an ask for money.
- Make sure your marketing materials (digital included) demonstrate that you not only recognize DAFs and are happy to work with them, but also that you're aware of the rules governing their use.

- Take a look at the checks you receive. Recently, a friend who sits on the board of one of the charities I support called to thank me for a gift *and* to enquire about the other name on the check. That other name was the organization that houses my DAF. Which means that not only did this friend learn about DAFs during our call, she also learned about me as a donor. Why? Because as donors, we *choose* the institutions that house our funds, and there are many options. Fundraisers who pay attention to these choices gain valuable insight into the donors who make them.
- Discuss DAFs with anyone you know who expects to come into money or is newly affluent. I can't get over the number of wealthy people who still write checks to charities one donation at a time. For them, discovering a streamlined option for their contributions, which is also cost-effective – well, that might be a really big deal. And who knows, your newly wealthy friend could one day express his gratitude for the introduction by directing contributions to *your* organization.
- Celebrate the efficiency of DAFs, and leverage it, too. I contribute to my DAF (technically, I recommend a contribution) from my iPhone. Often, I'm sitting right in front of a fundraiser and I get confirmation of the donation immediately, which I can share during the course of our conversation. Imagine if charities were to get strategic about how easy contributing is via a DAF, and use it to their advantage?

- If you can afford it, open your own DAF to experience how they work firsthand. The minimum contribution might surprise you.

FIVE

INVESTING BEYOND THE DOLLAR

The Risks and Rewards of Donor Participation

The research is clear. When donors volunteer, they feel better and give more. Yet many organizations cloister their donors to safeguard themselves and their staff from bad behavior, which can range from unreasonable donor demands to out-and-out power plays. If that weren't worrisome enough, just as many organizations swing the other way, pandering to their bossiest donors (or those with the biggest bank accounts) by letting them run the show.

This chapter offers an antidote to any fears you may be harboring about donor participation. I hope it inspires you. Because with all the attitude, entitlement, and demands donors bring – believe me, I see it too – it's easy to forget that they also bring wisdom, connections and skills to the organizations they support.

Of course, support (and I *do* mean financial support) is the operative word. Donors give more when they volunteer. According to Fidelity Charitable's study 'Time and Money:

The Role of Volunteering in Philanthropy,' volunteer donors give a remarkable *ten times* the amount that non-volunteers give. These volunteer donors are also more satisfied with the experience of giving, which can't help but bode well for retention.

Already I'm sure you can see that, within the larger context of philanthropy, this chapter is definitely no sidebar. That same Fidelity Charitable study found that 79% of donors, no matter the context, are also volunteers. Reportedly, these volunteer donors give of their time because they *want* to support the charities that they care about with more than just their wallet, which is an important donor insight.

But do charities welcome them?

Not often enough. My development-director friend Margot puts it down to a difference in mindset. She says, 'There are some organizations and some philanthropists that don't do well together because they don't have the same vision of what a partnership looks like. I've been part of many charities that have said "no" to donors because those donors were controlling. They had their own vision.'

Which brings us to something of a delicate matter.

Rich People are Crazy

Yes, they are.

I remember the first time I saw a board member screaming at a development professional. I went to the head of the organization immediately, and this was her response: 'Lisa, she screams at me all the time.'

'You let her get away with it?' I asked.

'She's a very big donor.'

It was that cut and dried. And in case you think it's cultural – that the diva thing is okay in LA – it isn't. It's never okay.

When Josh and I are hosting charitable events at our home, we constantly get vendors and caterers asking us where they're 'allowed' to go to the bathroom. '*Allowed?*' I always ask, wondering who made them feel so unworthy. Then I show them to the nearest bathroom, which is the same bathroom used by my family. Each and every time, they look about as shocked by the exchange as I am.

Even my friends north of the border have stories. Despite Canada's reputation for excessive courtesy, the country's donors appear to be just as ready to be rude when it suits them. Or pushy, as Hélène – a development professional at a Toronto charity – realized, when she was instructed by her superiors to allow a disagreeable (but major) donor to completely rewrite the charity's mission statement. And redo its logo. This was a charity that had existed for decades.

Then there's the donor who insisted her gift go toward the creation of a tranquillity garden, which staff members themselves would have to care for, since there was no money in the budget for upkeep. Or the many donors who lie about pledges, really messing with the bottom line of the organizations they claim to support.

Academia is rife with these anecdotes too. Sheila (who first appeared in Chapter Three) has a story about a donor who endowed a professorship at an important American university. 'Where's my professor?' the donor asked, about a week after making his gift. 'I want you to announce my professor!' He continued in this vein, badgering university staff until someone had to tell him that academic process is a thing, and it exists for a reason. It turns out that the donor wanted a friend of his to assume the role of the endowed professorship, and he was furious when he realized he couldn't make that happen.

Speaking of academia, remember the Harvard University tour that I described in Chapter Two? Well, our student guide regaled us with another story specific to donors, this one about the Widener Library. The library's namesake, Harry Elkins Widener, died on the *Titanic* when he was just twenty-seven. While a student at Harvard, Widener had started a rare-book collection that would eventually include first-edition copies of works by Charles Dickens, Robert Louis Stevenson, and other literary notables. After Widener's death, his grieving mother Eleanor (one of the few who survived the *Titanic*'s sinking) gifted his alma matter with $2M. This is equivalent to $70M in today's money, and was enough to build the library that would eventually house her son's collection.

What's relevant here is that the gift came with strings, which have become the stuff of legend at Harvard in the century since the library's construction. False stories abound; for example, that swimming lessons are a precondition of graduation from the university (because of Harry's death by drowning) or that ice cream must be perpetually available to Harvard students (because it was Harry's favorite treat). Neither of these stories is true. Eleanor Widener did have demands: namely, that Harvard use the architects of her choice and that it complete the library exterior according only to her tastes. But the fact that people *believe* the Widener myths (and discuss them to this day) says an awful lot about how very badly we expect donors to behave.

Sadly, it only takes one bad apple to ruin it for the good ones.

Charities Are Choosing Between Bad and Worse

As we've seen, donors often want to give or volunteer on their own terms, and that's not always what an organization needs. So, charities tend to shield their donors or pander to them, and the upshot is that no one wins.

This is part of the complexity of donor/fundraiser relationships, some of which we explored in Chapter Three. When I asked my fundraiser friend Linda about the challenges she's experienced with volunteer donors, she put it this way: 'When there have been issues, underlying each of them is a problematic power dynamic between the funders and the organization, which often makes funders believe that they can shape the narrative.'

The problem is that, for many donors, being shielded from the narrative – for example, by being cloistered away from the action and/or only ever being privy to an organization's 'marketing' story – is alienating. As donors, if we know we're being 'handled,' and we *always* know, we're far less likely to stick around.

Conversely, organizations that pander to donors by letting them, as Linda says, 'shape the narrative' – or assume responsibilities and functions that they're not qualified to carry out – are dangerous. What about the integrity of organizational mission? This is an issue we'll explore in detail in Chapter Six's conversation about governance.

To make matters worse, alternatives to these two approaches, though well-meaning, can be problematic too. Here's Margot's take: 'In the last decade, I have donors who have increased their giving, and they're constantly telling me that they don't feel engaged. No matter what I do, it's this perpetual story of not feeling engaged. So I give them a project. I ask them to help, for example, with donor stewardship. And *when* I ask, they're very agreeable. But then they come back midway through, wanting to abandon the task and do something else. Or they suddenly treat me like an adversary because they've started to feel that they own the project and that, as a leader, my agenda conflicts with it. So, the whole notion of collaborating with people who don't "work" for the institution directly but rather work through their volunteerism – it's challenging.'

Doing time as a donor – really gathering experience in the world of philanthropy – also matters. Margot talks about emerging philanthropists who hold unrealistic expectations about how much impact they'll have, not only with their monetary gifts, but also with the time they invest in the charities they support. 'Often they want to partner with you,' Margot says. 'They really want to take things to the next level. Which is great. Hopefully you're aligned and can do that. But usually you're performing a kind of emergency triage internally. You're trying to keep the fluids in the body of the organization, which is operating on a shoestring. You're trying to keep the patient from bleeding out. That's a hard thing to pair with a "next level" partnership.'

It *is* hard, but it isn't impossible. We'll get to what's great about donor participation momentarily. In the meantime, remember Ted (see pages 127–8) and his experience at the Rotary Club? As a Millennial himself, Ted is convinced that today's younger donors will only ever give if they can also engage. So, the risk, with the emerging philanthropists that Margot describes, is that they'll just go elsewhere. And, for better or worse, that's exactly what's happening.

The Kids Are Doing It for Themselves

Obviously, I'm poking fun with this subtitle, since few emerging donors are actually children. But I'm also making a point. If old-school philanthropy doesn't adapt to meet the needs of the next generation, that next generation will either leave the old school, or create a new one entirely. Again, 1 in 10 members of Generation Z reportedly want to start a charity themselves, so this really is an issue that we have to confront.

Stefanie Rhodes, CEO of Slingshot (whose mandate it is to mobilize younger funders), has spoken to me about donor engagement and the sector's future. She says, 'We all know the transfer of wealth is coming. We also all know that at some point, when the older generation steps back and these folks inherit the money, *they're* going to be our leaders and supporters. So, this is the moment to engage them, but it will require a recalibration of the system.'

Slingshot acts as a guide and catalyst for young Jewish philanthropists. And Stefanie's perspective, which reflects her time preparing the next generation to be leaders, is spot on. She says, 'The older generations can't possibly understand how to engage this group without also engaging the way they think and connect and the tools and technology they use.' Not doing so, she explains (for example, by failing to include younger donors as board members, even as you claim to value their opinions), will invariably make all your other efforts to engage seem inauthentic. 'And authenticity is what it's all about with them.'

Stefanie insists that plenty of opportunities exist to engage younger donors. 'But taking advantage of these opportunities requires an appetite for risk,' she says. An appetite, I might add, that rarely exists among traditional organizations. The good news is that risk tolerance can be developed. For these organizations, even authenticity of intention – or being upfront about how you hope to involve your youngest donors – is important. It's a great way to discover what those donors are about, and what they themselves might want their participation to look like.

It's also helpful to examine how Millennials are leading (already!) and what attitudes they bring to the work that they do. Take my young friend Rachel Sumekh. As founder and CEO of Swipe Out Hunger, Rachel's work has been recognized by the Obama White House and *The New York Times*. Her 2017 appearance on *Forbes* '30 Under 30' list puts her firmly in the demographic in question. It's people like Rachel we might look to learn from.

Swipe Out Hunger started in 2010 as a project among friends at UCLA. It's now the leading nonprofit addressing hunger among college students in the US. 'I got to UCLA,' explains Rachel, 'having barely volunteered a day in my life. And then my friend [and Swipe Out Hunger co-founder] Bryan Pezeshki posted something on Facebook along the lines of the following: "Let's donate the extra money on our meal plans to fight hunger. Message me if you're interested." All I could think was, that's really cool.'

'During our time at UCLA, it was just as Bryan proposed. We were able to convince people in the administration that it wasn't fair for them to be using unspent meal dollars as revenue – which was common practice on college campuses – when there were so many students struggling to even have access to that food.'

WHAT'S PERSONAL ABOUT PHILANTHROPY FOR RACHEL SUMEKH

At the end of the day, giving is always personal. Here's how Rachel (who is the child of Iranian Jewish immigrants) describes what got her involved:

Whereas the focus in the West is on the individual, Iranian culture is extremely tribal. If everyone is your responsibility growing up, as is the case in Iranian culture, you feel a real sense of urgency when you see someone suffering. The same is the case when you see an opportunity to help. Also, Iranians are known for being hospitable. If they offer you a piece of cake and you say 'no', they'll urge you three more times to take the cake.

So, I guess I learned not to see boundaries between myself and the person next to me. Instead, I see responsibility. It makes talking to donors very easy. When I meet donors, for example, I often hug them. I bring my same sense of warmth and intimacy. People say, 'You're first generation, you're a female founder – how hard has that been and what obstacles have you had to overcome?' That's not how I think of it at all. I see my identities as an asset.

That Rachel has learned to see beyond obstacles and focuses on mission is what I love about her approach to philanthropy. In my view, the warmth she describes when she meets a donor – she might as well be saying, 'take the cake!' – is exactly what this sector needs.

Rachel and Bryan's fledgling UCLA initiative has become a flagship program and national movement. Known today as 'The Swipes Drive,' the program enables students with extra dining hall meal swipes (which are the equivalent of 'meals' loaded on to a student or debit card) to donate them to their peers. More than 100 colleges are involved, and more than 2 million meals have been served to food-insecure students to date.

It's pretty remarkable. As you know, I'm interested in the practice and expression of philanthropy, as well as its benefits. Given that, what I love about Swipe Out Hunger's Swipes Drive is how enabling it is, for those who want to help. Also, how little it relies on money. Rachel, who started her career as a case manager, basically gives others the tools to achieve their own success. She says, 'A core value of ours is the belief that we're going to end hunger by leveraging resources that already exist. I came to the idea through Bryan, but a lot of other people had it, too. Students had always been sharing meal plans. We built the nonprofit to help proliferate the idea more effectively.

'I think the old model in nonprofits is "we'll come to you; we'll bring the panacea."' An example of this is the manner in which United Way used to work. The new model is the opposite. It assumes that you, as a person invested in creating change, *see* the challenge. Maybe you've even faced the challenge at some point and you're powerful and resilient enough to help to address it.'

Again, the lesson here is not about giving donors what they want – or, for the purposes of this chapter, appealing on an 'engagement' level to younger donors. Rather, it's about *rethinking* engagement, so that it services the mission directly, perhaps even becoming the reason that people get involved with an organization in the first place.

Is it generational? I ask Rachel. Does this approach only work with the young? 'Not at all,' she insists. 'Some of my favorite partners and collaborators are people in their fifties and sixties, and some are in their teens.'

So, what about the donor with unreasonable demands? 'That type of donor just doesn't get involved,' she says. 'Swipe Out Hunger is not a donor-focused organization. We're an issues organization. Because of that, I'm going to court donors who want to ask me the tough questions, the questions that make us better. And there are lots of those donors around.'

Clearly, Rachel's no-fear, no-pandering-to-donors attitude works. Under her watch, Swipe Out Hunger has expanded into other forms of student advocacy as well as policy creation, with she and her colleagues helping to author and pass $20M in student-focused legislation. Given that the organization itself is young – it turned ten in 2020 – I suspect that they're just getting started.

PHILANTHROPY, VOLUNTEERING, AND CIVIC ENGAGEMENT

Loosely defined, civic engagement is a broad set of practices and attitudes of involvement in social and political life, which together better the health of a democratic society. Philanthropy is thus a big part of civic engagement, as is volunteering. So how do today's trends in philanthropic engagement – particularly among young people – reflect what's happened to our civic institutions? Do we think differently today than we used to?

Alan Solomont is the Pierre and Pamela Omidyar Dean of the Jonathan M. Tisch College of Civic Life at Tufts University. He's also an entrepreneur, a philanthropist, and a political activist. But he doesn't have the easy answers. He told me, 'American democracy has always relied on robust civic institutions. This was the case from the beginning, even before the creation of the Republic. Ben Franklin, for example, started a volunteer fire department in Philadelphia in 1736, because the city's wood-framed houses were burning down.

'If you were to fast forward to the 70s, you'd find really strong civic institutions in the form of labor unions and church organizations and daily newspapers (all of which had the same headline, or at least the same facts) as well as universities and hospitals. It was through these institutions that we learned about democracy, and how to work with one another in a democratic context. There was also less income inequality in relative terms, and everyone learned civics in school.

'But between then and now, for a lot of different reasons, those civic institutions have been weakened, if not eliminated. We're not reading the same newspaper or watching the same network on televisions. Labor unions are weak and church attendance is down. People learn about democracy through doing and volunteering, participating in things like church suppers. That's civic life. So, this is a real period of transition for civic life, and we have yet to figure out what we need.'

Alan might as well be saying, *stay tuned*. Which is interesting – not only in the context of this conversation about engagement, but also as we look to philanthropy's future. He strikes me as hopeful, however. For example, he's eager to talk about the 2016 pre- and post-election polling he was involved in, which focused on the attitudes of American youth. He says, 'There is a great belief among young people that if they work together, they *can* make change.'

Donor Participation: How We Move from Risk to Reward

My first piece of advice is simple. Nonprofits, you need to recognize the difference between engaging donors and pleasing them. If it's helpful, acknowledge the power dynamic we discussed in Chapter Three. But also understand that, if you say no to donors who have unreasonable demands about the nature of their involvement in your organization, it's not the end of the world. Maybe you get ahead of the situation by creating suitable opportunities for those donors to be involved in the future? As we're about to discuss, really knowing your donors will help you do that.

ASKING THE BIG QUESTIONS TO BETTER POSITION VOLUNTEERS

The inclination model, which many fundraisers use when they're trying to establish a prospect's propensity (or inclination) to give and their relative affinity with a cause, can also be applied to donor engagement. As we discussed in Chapter Three, Lilly Family School of Philanthropy's Timothy Seiler suggests that we ask donors big questions regarding their philanthropic ambitions. Why not use these questions to figure out how to better engage your donors as volunteers?

On the topic of donor/fundraiser relationships and exploring what donors want aspirationally from their philanthropic work, Timothy told me: 'Another open-ended question for fundraisers to ask their donors is, "What would you most like to see this organization do in regard to your philanthropy?" Which is risky, because if the donor wants to do something that's not consistent with your organization's mission, you've got a difficult situation that you now have to negotiate. But that's the level of sophistication we strive for in relationships, where we're matching donor interests with organizational interests.'

It *is* risky, but it's not without reward. Taking Timothy's advice (asking donors the really meaty questions regarding what's meaningful personally about their own philanthropy) will help clarify if, for example, donors are in the game simply to write a check and feel good about themselves, or to exercise their skills as consultants, or host charitable events, or work in a hands-on way with communities in need.

I appreciate how hard it can be for fundraisers to let go of the desire to please, especially where money is involved. The fact is, when big donors want an organization to do something, even if that thing is insane, they tend to get their way. Getting *between* them and their way takes courage.

And yet successful people, in my experience, are *great* at

saying no. They say it and commit to it, or they turn their 'no' into an opportunity. Either way, they say it.

I have a lot of admiration for the fundraisers I know who are perfectly okay with their 'failure' to get money out of me. What they all seem to share is a level of comfort with rejection. Maybe they're playing the long game, hoping to win me over down the road. The point is, because they're comfortable going in, confident in what's right for their cause, they only want a 'yes' from me if I'm *also* right for the cause. The exchange is genuine. And this means we can still build a relationship, if that's in the cards. Even after I've said 'no.'

My friend Joel Braunold is one such admirable fundraiser. Joel served for years as Executive Director of the Alliance for Middle East Peace, and here's how he describes one of our early conversations: 'I remember sitting with Lisa and asking her: "Would you consider a gift?" Her response was, "My giving in this particular category goes through another organization." And I said, "Okay, good to know." And that was that.'

For Joel, my 'no' was a pivot. It moved us to a different sort of relationship than the one he had anticipated. Was it awkward? 'It meant,' Joel says, 'that Lisa understood the relationship I had been wanting with her and Josh. It also made clear that there was no financial end point. To me, that [point] was irrelevant. It's wonderful to socialize with Lisa and Josh. They're amazing hosts and they have a real ability to be connectors. I no longer have any aspirations for them to give but I do feel connected to them, and I know we'll have a friendship regardless.'

USING DONORS AS CONNECTORS

One of my fundraiser friends has a saying: 'The very best thing a donor can do is bring me five other donors.'

This is really about widening the net, and whether it means we prevail upon donors to act as ambassadors for the organizations they support (which should be a given) or we become much more open to donors bringing a friend (or five) to the charitable events they attend – it's important.

Social capital is capital. And yet the thinking around events (high-end fundraisers in particular, though this can also apply to modest gatherings) is never 'How can I get this donor to bring five other guests?' Instead, fundraisers invite 'vetted' guests that they have already determined are prospects. Their organization lacks the resources, they say, to look into anyone new. But how do they think that time-shares are sold?

Friends or acquaintances is how. And those of us willing to share them are advocates for our organizations – we're just engaging in 'work' of a sort that is more indirect. I love being a connector, and I've seen the payoff in so many other industries. You just have to believe that the dots will connect … maybe when you least expect it and in absolutely the best way possible.

Joel Braunold sees me as a connector and he's also my friend. I'm good with that because it's honest. 'Was I disappointed with the outcome?' Joel asks, referring again to his pitch. 'Sure. But that's the way of the world. Not everyone is going to give. For me, it's still personally and professionally meaningful to invest in Lisa and Josh because they're interesting. They're lovely people. If I've got a dollar amount that I need to hit, I know it's not going to come through them. So sometimes I can't prioritize them over a meeting that might lead to a gift. But if I have time or if they can host me, I always try to see them. As a nonprofit professional especially, I know that relationships last. In Josh and Lisa's case, I may go on and do something else in my career, and it may or may not be up their alley.'

The 'something else' Joel refers to is important. As a donor, I've also had to deal with the dreaded 'no.' I've had to pivot, and the results were better than I could have hoped. Remember how Big Sunday's David Levinson reacted to my 'brilliant' idea, the one I described in Chapter One? Here's a recap:

'David,' I said, as we finished our meeting, 'Josh and I want to feed every hungry person in Los Angeles for three months. What would it cost?'

'Let me work on that,' he said. 'I'll get back to you.'

A few days later I asked again, 'David, what's it going to cost?'

'I'm not going to tell you,' he said.

'Excuse me?'

'Lisa, it's irrelevant. It's a bad idea because it's not sustainable. You feed everyone for three months and then what? What happens in month four?'

He was respectfully saying no, and I was listening. As they say, the rest is history.

Volunteering

'No one is more surprised than me,' David Levinson tells me today, when reflecting on Big Sunday's history. Part of that history involved a career move that took David from Hollywood, where he was thriving as a writer, to communities in need. He would eventually become the 2009 California Nonprofit Leader of the Year. 'I lived in the same world as a lot of our donors,' he says, when describing Big Sunday's success. 'This made it much easier. Not only was I able to meet people as a peer, I'd also been on the other side. I'd had people coming to me and asking for money, and I knew what worked.'

David's ability to say 'no' to donors, as he demonstrated so well with me, is just the tip of the iceberg when it comes to what works. Big Sunday is hands down the best example I know of effective volunteer programming. The organization's mandate is to connect people through helping. Its core value, that 'absolutely everyone has some way that they can help somebody else,' is evinced in the 2,000 opportunities for volunteer involvement that it offers annually – everything from service and employment projects to the collection of materials for food, book, and school supply drives.

What Josh and I support (see pages 45–6) is Big Sunday's End of the Month Club, a food drive that evolved out of my initial conversation with David. The initiative got its name from the shortage that's experienced at food banks toward the end of each month, when many people of limited means have used up all their money and need extra help to feed their families.

In working with David, I've realized that much can be learned from his egalitarian approach to volunteer engagement. He stays focused on the issue – food insecurity, in this case – as well as how empowering it can be (for everyone!) to address it. I suspect he's got zero time for donor histrionics.

David says, 'The process of filling the food bags by bringing together a diversity of people is as important as getting the bags out there. We like to blur the lines between giving and receiving, so some of the people filling bags are receiving them as well.'

Big Sunday is also open to what its supporters bring to the table. For example, if you don't want to engage with the organization *this* way – because you lack the money, the skills or the time – here are 1,999 alternatives. It's a fabulous model, and one worth considering for any nonprofits seeking to engage supporters for the first time, or to better position existing volunteers.

'For our monthly collection,' David explains, 'we do peanut butter and jelly month, pasta and sauce month, and so on. We team up with strategic partners – a school or a business – to get it done. A talent agency, for example, did peanut butter and jelly month; our staff didn't even run it. We had high-powered agents out there collecting peanut butter!

'My favorite End of the Month Club experience came out of a call we got from a Catholic girls' school. "Could you guys collect?" we asked. And the teacher said, "That's not going to work. This school serves a low-income community." But the world is full of haves and have mores, we've all got a way to help, and so I went to the school myself. It was pasta and sauce month. I brought three bags of pasta with me, held them up, and told the kids that what we needed to collect were 100 bags. "At the 99-Cents store," I said, "these bags are three for a dollar. That's $0.33 each. I'll buy the first three, which means that you'll need to find me ninety-seven more."

'Two weeks later, three of the sincerest – and nerdiest – girls I've ever seen showed up at the office. We needed a trolley to bring in all the stuff they'd collected. They were so proud of themselves, and that's the point. We're in it together.'

UNDERSTANDING THE TYPES OF VOLUNTEER ENGAGEMENT

Broadly speaking, there are five different types of volunteer engagement:

Formal: Here, volunteers are scheduled into what is typically ongoing 'work.' Depending on the nature of what the volunteers have committed to do, they may receive training beforehand (for example, in a hospital setting, or for front-of-house volunteers in a theater) and they may also be supervised.

Informal: Individually driven, this sort of volunteer work usually happens outside of an organizational context. It's basically about good old helping, but it might involve beneficiaries that are not known personally to the volunteer (for example, in the case of neighbors who organize a meal-delivery service for a crossing guard who's fallen ill).

Project-based: Here, a volunteer's work ends when the project is done. This type of volunteering is common in the sector and includes, for example, certain aspects of charitable event planning or time-specific fundraising drives.

Social action: Again, there is a lot of crossover here with fundraising, as volunteers typically get involved as a means of advocating for a specific cause. Examples include political lobbying, the gathering of petition signatures, campaigning for environmental causes, and so on.

Governance: This type of volunteer work involves the provision of leadership and direction to an organization, and often involves board or committee service. We'll discuss it in detail in Chapter Six.

For the purposes of this book, what distinguishes volunteering from consulting (which we're about to discuss) or board participation (which we'll discuss in the next chapter) is really the fact that volunteering is open to everyone. Or at least it should be, if organizations are savvy enough to engage their communities. As a person with means and an extensive network, I look at the resources available to me and volunteer accordingly – whether it's by offering my services as a 'connector' or opening up our house (as we do several dozen times a year) to charitable events.

As David Levinson says, the important thing to remember is that 'absolutely everyone has some way that they can help somebody else.'

VOLUNTEERING DONE RIGHT:
CEDARS-SINAI MEDICAL CENTER

My philanthropist friend Lauren Kurzweil is effusive about nonprofits that deliver meaningful opportunities for volunteer engagement. She says: 'Cedars is the gold standard. Everything they do, they do well. They make people feel wanted, needed, and appreciated, which is very motivating. And when they ask you to do something, they provide parameters. Because the experience doesn't require you to go outside these parameters, it makes it easy to get the job done.

'Cedars hosted a one-day event, a healthcare "college" that enabled guests to attend seminars to learn about different medical issues. Members of the Cedars Board of Governors were invited to join a planning committee for this event, with each of us picking and interviewing a doctor and then introducing that doctor at the event itself. We had everything we needed: the doctors' contact details, a date by which we had to have reached them, interview questions, guidelines for writing our one-minute intros, and a clear deadline.

'Because Cedars took care of all the details, I felt I benefited personally from being part of the planning committee. I had a hand in deciding what topics we would cover at the conference and what doctors we would involve. It wasn't one of those situations where no one cared really about committee-member opinions or where everything had been decided in advance. It was really interesting.

'I also volunteer in the hospital emergency room and, for that, Cedars offers a lot of training. The training is all about what you can and can't do. So when you walk through the door as a volunteer, you're ready to perform. We greet patients, tell them where to go to triage, assist visitors in finding their loved ones – all to help ease some of the stress associated with having to be in the emergency room. Some people want blankets or food; some need a hand to hold. Whatever it is, we try to make their stay as good as it can be.'

Consulting

If one of your organization's major donors – someone who, while lovely, has never worked a day in her life – offers to put together the budget for your capital campaign, what do you do? In no other sphere would you hire her, right? So, you have to be brave enough to say, for example, 'Thanks for the offer. We already have a number of people with the expertise that this requires. They'll be working on it with us. Why don't we find another way for you to be involved?'

The fear, of course, is that the lovely donor pulls her money. It probably won't happen, but it could. What's best for the organization – and I'm talking mission, not dollars – still has to come first.

I've seen a lot of organizations 'go stealth' about the every-day conducting of business because they don't want to get into a situation like this (where they feel beholden to the whims of a donor) in the first place. I've also seen development directors forbid their donors (even prospective ones) from speaking to staff.

It's a terrible shame. Because what those organizations lose, when they attempt to cloister their donors or prevent their involvement, is access to every good thing that those donors have to offer.

WHEN THE GIRL SCOUTS WOULDN'T LET BOARD MEMBERS BE MENTORS

Back when I served on the Girl Scouts' board, I received a call from someone on staff. 'Could you help us find mentors for a group of award-winning girls?' this person asked. 'Sure!' I responded. Then she elaborated: the Girl Scouts was holding an annual event to honor 100 young women out of the 40,000 or so who make up its membership. Basically, each of the girls being honored for her leadership was to be matched with a mentor – someone who'd found success in the field to which the girl aspired. The idea was that the chosen mentor would meet with the honoree before the event to share stories and offer career advice.

Sounds great, right? I thought so, especially since many members of the board matched perfectly, career-wise, with the ambitions of the girls being honored. Unfortunately, however, board members weren't allowed to be mentors. And while I still love the organization – and want to be involved with it – I can't help but file this experience under 'What Not to Do, Ever.'

Much of my own investment beyond the dollar has included commission and board service. In this way, I've supported dozens of organizations, everything from the Beverly Hills Cultural Heritage Commission to the Make-a-Wish Foundation. Often, by way of my role on these boards, I've also consulted. Sometimes I'll support a nonprofit whose mandate appeals to me (but whose board I have nothing to do with) by consulting, too. If the fit is right, it's always worthwhile.

Here's an example. I sit on the international Board of Directors for the New Israel Fund (NIF). My board colleagues and I saw a presentation recently that didn't go over too well. The staff member delivering the presentation was very senior, and she became visibly frustrated when she realized she was tanking. I went up to her afterward and said, 'Look, if you'd like help with this, I'm more than happy to work with you.'

The staff member was a little uncertain, probably about the appropriateness of my involvement. So, I spoke with Daniel Sokatch, NIF's CEO, expressing my desire to help her directly.

'Would that be alright?' I asked. And Daniel said, 'Are you kidding? Yes!' After which point, the woman and I met. We conducted a full strategic analysis together and she went on to do better the next time. *She* benefited, NIF benefited, and I felt great. To this day, I feel infinitely more involved with the organization.

Josh's experience has also been interesting. I get that I'm biased, but even the evidence (namely, the revolutionizing of 3D cinema) shows that he is a technological genius. So, if you're an organization Josh supports and you're working for a cause about which he is passionate – I'm going to use the very personal example of Crohn's disease – how do you involve him in a way that's meaningful for everyone?

I've already introduced Dr. Dermot McGovern, the Joshua L. and Lisa Z. Greer Chair in Inflammatory Bowel Disease Genetics at Cedars. Calling Josh 'the most involved donor we have,' Dermot describes the beginning of their relationship this way: 'Initially, Josh said he'd be happy to come into the lab and wield the pipette [a tool used in chemistry, biology, and medicine to transport a measured volume of liquid]. My response was to tell him, "Look, you've got these amazing areas of expertise. If you really want to help out on the science side, using that expertise would be a great way to start." Josh had ideas, for example, about looking at DNA from a third perspective – that is, moving the science into a mature coupling with Big Data. We weren't in a place where we could take advantage of those ideas, but they are something we might return to in the future.

'It's about skill sets,' Dermot continues. 'The donor is providing an important resource, a financial resource, so of course there's sensitivity. But why would I want Josh to wander around the lab wielding a pipette when he has these amazing insights into technology? Also, he *wants* to develop those insights. So, as we finish our analysis of the data sets, we hope to be going back to him. I think this will come full circle.'

TAPPING THE EXPERTISE OF YOUR DONORS

There are as many ways of consulting as there are skill sets lurking in your donors. For example, the donors I know have collective experience in:

- Technology
- Strategy
- Business systems
- Government relations
- Health advocacy
- Partnerships and collaboration
- Grant applications
- Human resources and recruitment
- Leadership training
- Marketing and communications
- Design thinking
- Finance
- Purchasing and sourcing
- Taxation
- Governance, risk, and compliance

These people are more than happy to lend their expertise to the organizations they support – so why not look for a similar knowledge base in yours? I suspect you'll be surprised to learn that donors who appeared not to want to get their hands dirty via traditional donor volunteer work will happily roll up their sleeves when their 'heads' are involved. That's consulting, and for charities (as well as the skilled donors who support them), it's worth its weight in major gifts.

SIX

WHAT MONEY CAN'T BUY

*Trust, Good Governance,
and Better Boards*

More than once, I have walked away from charitable organizations for reasons of principle. I've done it even when I believed in the good work they were doing.

Financial misdeeds, discrimination, and harassment are never okay – whether they involve development professionals or donors. This chapter examines the importance of functioning with honesty and transparency and dealing openly with wrongdoing or scandal. It also looks at the role of board-member donors, clarifying the ever-important relationship between a good board and good governance.

How Not to Measure a Charity

Nonprofits face less scrutiny than organizations in healthcare, government or even industry, probably because they benefit from a presumption of virtue. So how do donors make informed decisions about where to direct their charitable dollars? How do they find organizations they can trust?

Often, prospective donors will visit a charities rating platform. (As you're probably aware, DAF sponsors will visit them, too, when they need to confirm that a charity is legitimate.) In the USA, our go-to websites for ratings are Charity Navigator and GuideStar. But there are others, such as CharityWatch, and there are also equivalents in the UK and Canada. Unfortunately, none of them help me sleep at night.

Here's what Charity Navigator promises: 'Founded in 2001, Charity Navigator has become the nation's largest and most-utilized evaluator of charities. In our quest to help donors, our team of professional analysts has examined tens of thousands of nonprofit financial documents. We've used this knowledge to develop an unbiased, objective, numbers-based rating system to assess over 9,000 of America's best-known and some lesser-known, but worthy, charities. Charity Navigator's rating system examines two broad areas of a charity's performance: their Financial Health and their Accountability & Transparency. Our ratings show givers how efficiently we believe a charity will use their support today, how well it has sustained its programs and services over time and its level of commitment to good governance, best practices, and openness with information.'

And this is what's on offer with GuideStar: 'GuideStar's Nonprofit Profiles provide you with the information you need to make smart decisions, build connections, and learn from each other to achieve your missions. We obtain data from public sources, other organizations that promote philanthropy, and the nonprofits themselves. We then aggregate it into GuideStar Nonprofit Profiles, one profile for each organization in our database. Every nonprofit on our site is invited to update its profile. There's no charge to update.'

The first problem with these ratings systems is that, while they claim (to quote Charity Navigator's website) to 'show givers how efficiently we believe a charity will use their support,' most of how they measure 'efficiency' comes down to money-for-operations versus money-for-cause, which of course we discussed in Chapters Three and Four. Obviously, it's important to ensure that a charity isn't overspending on administration. But, as a donor, I'd trust somebody who's making a decent living long before I'd trust the guy who is happy to work for free. Not to mention the fact that real efficiency should be measured in outcomes, not overhead – an issue we'll get into momentarily.

There's also the fact that our popular ratings platforms make comparative benchmarking a challenge. Charity Navigator and GuideStar are only able to include financial data gathered from charities required by law to complete a Form 990, which is the US information return specific to tax-exempt organizations. Places of worship, and certain organizations with a religious affiliation, are exempted from filing. Religious institutions don't even have to do an audit; they're asked only to complete a review, which is something of an 'audit-light' and therefore really not an audit at all. So any analysis offered by these ratings platforms is woefully inadequate from the get-go.

This doesn't even touch the issue of self-reporting. Form 990s are self-reported, and most small tax-exempt organizations whose annual gross receipts are $50,000 or less can satisfy annual reporting requirements by submitting data online. In larger organizations, one might expect the board to audit these 990 data, but it's still relatively easy for organizations to game the ratings system – for example, by moving stuff around (data that doesn't have tax implications but *does* affect a charity's 'score'). There is risk involved, sure, but only if you (or the IRS) were to go through this stuff with a fine tooth-comb. And that rarely happens in the charitable sector.

The Lilly Family School's Timothy Seiler also talks about how reductive it is to measure success in the charity sector based on numbers alone. Instead of public perception or ratings, his focus is on *internal* measures – or how organizations assess their fundraising staff. Still, what's interesting is what these measures leave out. Timothy tells me, 'Among fundraisers, performance is evaluated on the basis of the number of dollars they raise, and this sometimes forces them into the position of transactional fundraising. We do need to count dollars raised; it's part of fundraising. But there are other ways to measure success. Can we get to a place where we measure deepening relationships? Can we measure the number of new relationships? How about donor satisfaction and donor loyalty? These measures will move us more toward trusting and meaningful relationships and better fundraising and gift-giving.'

If I'm one of your prospects, who you are is as important to me as what you do, especially if what you do is only defined by your numbers. To Timothy's point, how 'good' you are at building meaningful relationships, for example, matters a great deal. Why wouldn't it? It shows me who you are and what we share – in terms of our philanthropic goals – and how, together, we might just achieve the remarkable.

SOMETIMES, OPTICS ARE A MEASURE TOO

After watching *The Crown* recently on Netflix, I decided to further satisfy my curiosity about Britain's royal family through the almost-as-bingeworthy 2017 documentary *The Royal House of Windsor*. Needless to say, it was fascinating. I happened to be writing this book at the time, and what particularly struck me was a comment by Dr. Piers Brendon, an historian interviewed in Episode Five.

'Charity has always been a secret weapon of the monarchy,' Brendon said.

Really?! I mean, I suppose I'm not surprised. You're about to read all sorts of stories about organizations and/or people whose good deeds – and charitable work – helped to establish their 'saintly' reputations and protect them from the consequences of scandal.

Brendon's comment, in *The Royal House of Windsor*, was actually made in reference to Diana, Princess of Wales, whose charitable habits were evidently not in line with

Queen Elizabeth II's choice to support 'uncontroversial' charities. And, according to Brendon, this was very good PR: 'Diana saw the possibility of getting much more publicity by dealing with lepers, by dealing with the maimed, by dealing with AIDS victims ...' so powerful was her challenge to established royal order.

How Not to Ask Charities to Measure Themselves

In philanthropy, the 'remarkable' is almost always about outcomes, and yet the sector struggles to measure – or effectively measure – impact. The impact revolution is a thing that I can definitely get behind as a donor. The problem is, these days I'm urged to give based only on impact to charities that measure their impact themselves. Whom do I trust?

Also, doesn't asking charities to provide evidence of impact unduly favor the ones (the big ones, typically) that can afford to pay for research? If you're a great charity with a staff of three and an incredibly limited budget, paying for an independent specialist to gather evidence of your impact – especially in a sector where no benchmarks for impact exist – is likely beyond your means. So what are you going to do? You're going to take one of your three staff members and task her with research. Then, your fundraising suffers. It doesn't make a whole lot of sense.

Despite these challenges, Charity Navigator started publishing impact information recently on its website. The information is 'gathered' via a collaboration among GuideStar, Classy, GlobalGiving, ImpactMatters, and Charity Navigator, and we're told that it doesn't affect a charity's 'score.' This is probably a good thing, since the impact information that's published is prepared by the charities themselves. Still, it's a step in the right direction, since at least they're considering impact as part of the equation. It's not yet a wholly *reliable* step – but it's a step, nonetheless.

It reminds me of the early Internet era. Those of us who worked in the industry (or around it) in its nascent days were all clamoring to find ways to measure *hits*, as we called them, or the number of visitors to a given website. Funder/investors wanted this information and reasonably so, because it spoke to a website's impact. But nobody knew where to start. No standards existed, so people provided numbers that were the product of guesswork. And since we lacked consistent metrics with which to measure and benchmark performance, these numbers were all over the map.

We got there, though. And philanthropy will, too.

IMPACT, BRAND PROMISE, AND TRUST

We've all heard stories about charities that fail to deliver on their promises. Each and every one of them damages the sector. Far worse, however, is when charities 'fudge' (or hide) their poor results in order to protect their 'good' reputations. As a donor, feeling disappointed over an organization's failure to deliver is one thing; feeling duped by a lie – even if it's a lie of omission – is another thing entirely.

Brand isn't so much about who you are as an organization, but who people *think* you are – and I sometimes worry that it matters more than the truth. It's why I believe we're all responsible for ensuring that honesty prevails in philanthropy. As a donor/board member, for example, I'm more than willing to speak up if I see something amiss. I consider this my fiduciary responsibility. And as sector leaders, I've got to believe that your honesty with donors (existing *and* prospective) is a given. They have every right to demand it.

Besides, most of today's donors realize that their financial support of a cause is a form of investment and should be treated as such. I'm fairly sure that you wouldn't expect us to invest in stock based only on brand reputation. On the contrary, we'd explore brand claims and collect evidence on performance and potential. Why should our charitable investments be any different?

Here's an example of a broken brand promise. Locks of Love, a nonprofit that urges folks to donate their own human hair for wig-making, was once a household name. It's been around since 1997 and it's got a four-star rating on Charity Navigator. But get this: Nonprofit Investor's analysis of the organization a few years ago revealed a remarkable $6M in unaccounted hair donations annually.

According to a much-discussed dissection of the analysis in *Forbes*, Locks of Love received 104,000 donations of hair in the sample year, 2011. Locks of Love has indicated that each hairpiece it makes requires 6–10 hair donations, but as much as 80% of hair donated to the organization is unusable. Even so, by those calculations, 104,000 hair donations should make 2,080 wigs – and only 317 wigs were produced in the sample year. Compare that to the Pantene Beautiful Lengths program, which (until it shuttered recently due to the rise in synthetic-hair technology) distributed more than 4,200 wigs annually based on average donations of 75,000 bundles of hair.

The organization disputes the donation figures. It turns out that Locks of Love, whose annual budget is based largely on individual donations, claims to have no tracking mechanisms for incoming hair. Purportedly, Locks of Love also has no knowledge of its ratios of incoming hair to wigs, to sales of hair to others. That's pretty abysmal record-keeping, which Marc Owens (the former director of the tax-exempt division of the IRS) confirms with this statement on the organization's financials to CBS San Francisco: 'There are just so many omissions, that it's hard to say for certain that any of the data on the return is accurate.'

Pretty shocking, right? Yet despite the reputational damage suffered by Locks of Love, it continues to be regarded as a 'viable' charity, likely because its cause – helping kids suffering hair loss for medical reasons via donated hair prosthetics – is undeniably worthy. Still, there have been consequences. *I* wouldn't give the organization my hair, and I know I'm not alone. In fact, since Locks of Love isn't the only brand in this philanthropic space, it might do well to consider partnering in the future with one of its better-run brand alternatives.

In the meantime, Locks of Love is a lesson. Obviously, brand matters. But delivering on brand promise, and being honest with your stakeholders when you can't, is everything.

Why Good Governance Matters to Giving

The values underpinning any philanthropic activity – generosity, responsibility, and trust, to name a few – make accountability in our sector integral. At the end of the day, we're dealing with other people's hearts and also their money.

Any breach in trust, therefore, is deadly. I have experienced more of these than I care to remember, but one of the most personally disappointing involved Morris Dees. An American lawyer and civil rights activist, Dees is known for founding the Southern Poverty Law Center (SPLC), an amazingly influential American nonprofit advocacy association.

Dees' name was always synonymous in my mind with doing good, fighting the KKK and other extremists, and with Rosa Parks. Why Rosa Parks? Because, many years ago, the Hollywood Women's Political Committee (which at the time included several hundred entertainment-industry power-houses ... and me) honored Morris Dees and Rosa Parks at its annual gala at the Beverly Wilshire Hotel. Ever since, Parks' autograph has been a proud part of our family archives, and I myself have slept better for the simple fact that she existed, and that Morris Dees was out there continuing to work for toler-ance and fight for justice. That is, until early 2019.

It all came crashing down for me when I read Bob Moser's scathing *The New Yorker* news story, 'The Reckoning of Morris Dees and the Southern Poverty Law Center.' In it, Moser, a former employee of the SPLC, insists that he speaks for his SPLC colleagues when he writes, 'We were part of the con, and we knew it.'

These are pretty harsh words, and they're not even the half of it. Basically, the SPLC fired Dees for undisclosed reasons prior to the article's publication. By way of explanation, Moser describes Dees in 'The Reckoning' as having a 'reputation for hitting on young women,' writing that his dismissal came 'amid a staff revolt over the mistreatment of non-white and female employees' by Dees and SPLC leadership, although Dees denies the allegations. Also, the SPLC, a nonprofit, took in so much money that it apparently ended up with more in its coffers than it could ever possibly spend – a situation that Moser claims led staff to nickname the organization the 'Poverty Palace.'

Donors like myself, who gave to the Poverty Palace, probably face a reckoning of their own, in this case, about whom they'll trust with their charitable dollars in the future. The risk is that they won't trust anyone, and if *they* stop giving and other donors join them, philanthropy as we know it falls apart.

You already know, of course, that this is something I worry about. I worry more about the sector with every new scandal. But I also have a lot of faith in the solution: good governance.

So, first, a definition. The Chartered Governance Institute (ICSA) in the UK provides visitors to its website with a simple summation: 'Corporate governance is the system of rules, practices and processes by which a company is directed and controlled. Corporate Governance refers to the way in which companies are governed and to what purpose. It identifies who has power and accountability, and who makes decisions.'

Pretty straightforward, right? And here's where trust comes in – again, per the ICSA: 'Governance at a corporate level includes the processes through which a company's objectives are set and pursued in the context of the social, regulatory and market environment. It is concerned with practices and procedures for trying to make sure that a company is run in such a way that it achieves its objectives, while ensuring that stakeholders can have confidence that their trust in that company is well founded.'

As you can see, good governance is just good business. Nonprofits *can* survive a hit to stakeholder trust, but doing so requires a rebuilding of the sort of confidence the ICSA describes, and that means holding those responsible for it accountable, being honest about it, and putting measures in place to ensure that it never happens again. Doing anything less hurts all of us – funders, fundraisers, and (most of all) everyone in need of our help.

THE NEW NORM?

Have you ever wondered if scandal in the sector is just the new norm? I know I have. But the more we talk about this stuff, the more likely we are, collectively, to insist that it never be tolerated.

Billionaire investor and philanthropist Michael Steinhardt is one of the largest donors in America today. A gallery in the Metropolitan Museum of Art's Greek wing is named after him and his wife; he co-founded Birthright Israel along with Charles Bronfman; and he's got his name on a school at NYU. It may *look* like he emerged unscathed from recent scandal, but history may not be as forgiving.

Here's what happened. According to a front-page article in *The New York Times* in 2019, six women allege that they were sexually harassed by Steinhardt. The article alleges these women had come to Steinhardt in their capacity as fundraisers or had relied on him in their work as rabbis in a fellowship he funded. A seventh woman filed a lawsuit containing similar claims, which in all cases allege Steinhardt made sexual remarks or requests of his accusers. Many claim they witnessed these sexual remarks, and it turns out that Steinhardt had previously been the subject of other such claims, appearing in two sexual harassment lawsuits filed in state court in Manhattan, in 2012 and 2013.

Steinhardt denied harassment and said he had never touched anyone inappropriately but did admit to making inappropriate remarks.

Many organizations voiced their support for the women who spoke out against Steinhardt. Many other organizations, however, remain silent to this day, and I have to wonder if there's a relationship here between dollars and their neutrality.

Birthright Israel continues to send thousands of kids on free trips to Israel. Also, NYU's Steinhardt School of Culture, Education, and Human Development announced in late 2019 that it will not be renamed, despite Steinhardt's admission of making inappropriate remarks. After *The New York Times* article was published, NYU designated a subcommittee to review the allegations against him, a process that included a solicitation for relevant information from the Steinhardt School community. But according to the blog NYU Local, an email was circulated to that community from the Board of Trustees (note that Steinhardt is himself a trustee), which stressed that the results of the review 'did not warrant renaming the school.'

Naturally, my fear is that the virtue we ascribe to philanthropists is really messing with our judgment. I fear that people like Steinhardt are counting on the fact that the good they do (and the charitable dollars they dispense) frankly outweighs the bad. And yet the global #MeToo movement against sexual harassment, which encourages 'breaking the silence,' continues to grow. The movement is about strength in numbers, and the more we discuss this type of unacceptable behavior in the philanthropic sector, the better our chances, collectively, of really 'living' the values that got us involved with giving.

Here, as everywhere else, our actions reflect those values. So, to the National Council of Jewish Women, who hired Steinhardt victim/accuser Sheila Katz as its CEO within a week of the Steinhardt story appearing in *The New York Times*, I say, well done. As a philanthropist, I'm paying attention.

We all are.

Why Boards Matter, Too

Boards matter. So much, in fact, that they warrant their own book – a project I might consider tackling down the road. In the meantime, let's take a look at board governance, because it's often misrepresented.

True nonprofit boards hold collective legal guardianship of the organizations they represent. They are responsible for ensuring that all available resources are used to fulfill the organization's purpose. They do this as a group and according to policy, since no individual board director should ever have separate authority. All board directors, however, hold fiduciary responsibility, which means that, not only are they responsible (again, collectively) for financial oversight; they're also tasked with ensuring that *all* resources (staff is a big one) are used effectively to service the organization's mission.

Most nonprofit board directors are volunteers, since profiting personally from the role would be a major conflict of interest. But there's also a fundraising element, and it's huge. Despite this, the 2017 National Index of Nonprofit Board Practices includes the following statement in its assessment of board performance: 'Both board chairs and executive directors identify fundraising as the weakest aspect of board performance, and research suggests a major driver is poorly established expectations for fundraising during board recruitment.'

THE GIVE/GET OF BOARDS

It used to be that boards were either 'give *or* get.' These days, however, almost all board members are required to make a personal donation as well as assist with fundraising. So 'give *and* get' is much more apt.

The particulars are tricky. Let's say a board is asking its members to commit, not so much to a prescribed amount, but to the height of their capacity individually. What about those members who bring incredible value but don't have capacity? How does the board monetize their contributions?

Then, too, consider the criticisms faced recently by some of our largest cultural institutions. In the October 2019 *New York Times* article 'New Scrutiny of Museum Boards Takes Aim at World of Wealth and Status,' the writers report on the pressure that exists to make the boards of these institutions representative of the communities they serve. But the Museum of Modern Art, for example, estimates that its trustees contribute as much as 20% of its $175M budget. And at the Whitney, a new trustee 'is generally expected to contribute about $5M within a few years of joining the board, and then about $200K annually to stay on it.' The article identifies the finance industry as the source of the wealth of some 40% of this type of board member, with real estate and energy being sources too – so there's no way that these folks are representative of their communities.

The thing is, organizations run on money. Every board member should be required to make a contribution, in my opinion, and where that's not possible for reasons of personal capacity, boards should accommodate a certain number of members based on skill. This could be a lawyer who offers his or her services pro bono, for example, or an academic; people whose qualifications will uniquely serve the cause. As for the 'get' part of the equation, or the fundraising: this should be a given. Otherwise, people like me – board members who fulfill their give/get requirements only to realize that others with capacity haven't – feel like chumps.

Poorly established expectations (and/or definitions of service) cause all sorts of problems on boards, not just those specific to fundraising. Even the word 'board' is used too broadly, and these days – at least in larger nonprofits – can be tacked on to all manner of volunteer-based entities ('executive boards' often, or 'sub-boards'), which for all intents and purposes are just committees. Some of these 'boards' have 100 members and no ability to make decisions, so it's no wonder that meeting attendance often hovers around 50%.

Then there are 'legacy' boards, with upward of 200 people. How do they get anything done? The short answer is that they don't. Typically, these monster boards exist because their members pay to be on them. And if you've got 250 members giving $5,000 a pop – well, you get the idea. 'Call them ambassadors,' I've suggested, 'to distinguish what they do from board governance.' But, as I've been told, people like being able to say that they're members of the board. So, organizations looking to please their supporters continue to offer them these 'fake' roles, and the pandering and inefficiency go on.

TRAINING YOUNGER DONORS TO
BE BOARD MEMBERS

A recent article in the *Harvard Business Review*, 'Why You Should Create a "Shadow Board" of Younger Employees,' reports that: 'A lot of companies struggle with two apparently unrelated problems: disengaged younger workers and a weak response to changing market conditions. A few companies have tackled both problems at the same time by creating a "shadow board" – a group of non-executive employees that works with senior executives on strategic initiatives.'

This is a step in the right direction, an effort, as the article explains, to 'leverage the younger groups' insights and to diversify the perspectives that executives are exposed to.' But I'm not sure it's enough. The reason? Our youngest donors are extraordinarily socially engaged. They want to be in relationships with the people who are doing the work: making the decisions that address the issues of today, and also define tomorrow for all of us. They want to be in the room.

Throwing these generations a rather patronizing olive branch, or otherwise tagging their insights as 'useful' but 'young,' will likely just piss them off. Far better is the approach adopted by Slingshot, the next-generation Jewish philanthropic organization that I introduced to you in Chapter Five. Established through the support of the Andrea and Charles Bronfman Philanthropies and run by Stefanie Rhodes, Slingshot offers a board-training program as one of its group of innovative offerings. In partnership with the Paul and Jenna Segal Foundation (PJSF) and 21/64 (founded by Sharna Goldseker), the purpose of this program is not only to engage younger board members, but also to prepare them for effective board leadership.

See the difference? Slingshot's approach isn't about optics (that is, *looking* like you're engaging younger donors) and it's also not opportunistic. Instead, it's about true leadership and the future of the sector. For example, graduates of the PJSF X 21/64 Board Leadership course are eligible to be matched with compatible boards. Slingshot also plans to offer opportunities for existing boards to learn about how they'll need to adapt in order to really nurture multi-generational board leadership.

No matter their age, it's useful to consider why people volunteer for boards in the first place, and what organizations really want from their service. I've seen individuals come forward with major gifts, but the price of these gifts is a seat on the board. Here, the donors offering the gifts wanted status or power or both. On the other hand, I've had board-member colleagues who were only there to make friends. I've also had the great privilege of working with board members whose passion for the organization compelled them to do more – and 'more' meant having a hand in how the organization was run, ensuring its financial health, and guiding its future. The latter, of course, is ideal.

Nonprofits have their own sets of motives regarding the 'profile' of those on their boards, and not all of them are pure. Money is a big one, for example, since every nonprofit needs money. Power is a motivator, too, and this is sometimes expressed when board members are chosen for their propensity to stay quiet or otherwise agree with the direction and/or decisions taken by the chief executive or executive director. Happily, most organizations are also looking for expertise on their boards. They're looking for people with networks, diversity and a range of perspectives (also, in some cases, a true representation of the communities they serve). Best of all, they're looking to be challenged by a board that will not only uphold mission, but also advance it.

BOARD MEMBER INVOLVEMENT IN BRIEF

What Happens	What I'd Like to See More of
You have money. Please join our board.	You are passionate about our mission. Please join our board.
Board members aren't expected to volunteer. Your board service is enough.	Please get involved. Here are some opportunities for you to engage directly with our mission.
Please don't talk to staff.	Our staff is available to help you learn about what we're doing and how things work. If there's something you'd like a staff member to do, or do differently, please speak with the executive director.

Again, please don't talk to staff.	This member of our staff needs a mentor. Who on the board has the skills to help with the issue?
We're so grateful you could be at this meeting. We won't keep you too long.	We're eager for you to contribute your wisdom and experience to this process, and to engage in meaningful conversations and decisions.
Everything is fine. The organization is doing great.	We're facing some significant challenges. This is what's going on, and here's where we could use your expertise.
We have hired consultants and lawyers and experts. We don't want to bother you with the details.	You're a pretty well-connected group. Is there anyone you can put us in touch with, in order to help us address these challenges?
Yes. Yes. Yes. The donor is always right.	I hear what you're saying. Here are the organization's needs and challenges. Let's find a way to meet everyone's needs.
Yes. Yes. Yes. The donor is always right.	Please don't talk to the staff that way. It makes it impossible for us to do our jobs.

Board Policy, Protocol and Principle

What's required for a board to be effective in upholding mission (and best case, advancing it) is a clear set of guidelines, which outlines an organization's expectations for service (including those related to fundraising) and which also includes a code of ethics. BoardSource is an invaluable resource that helps support and enhance board performance. But it's still incumbent upon *every* organization with an active board to tackle the complexities involved in, for one example, recruiting and training new members. (You'd be amazed how often nonprofits 'forget' about standard procedures when a new board member comes forward with money.)

Also, rarely are there mechanisms in place that facilitate the removal of board members who aren't suitable any longer for service. Sometimes a person has been around too long; maybe they played a hand in the organization's founding, but the mission has changed in ways that they don't care for or can't support – whatever the reason, boards need guidelines for dealing with this sort of issue and others.

Then, too, where governance bylaws exist, we've got to make sure we read them. And by 'we,' I mean board members *and* staff. Bylaws are routinely referenced in the boards I've been on, but few people are familiar with them. For example, when I became a member of the board of an established synagogue in the early 2000s, I wanted to get my hands on its bylaws. No one could find them. The document did turn up, and that's when I discovered a clause at the end of it pertaining to 'service,' which referred to what would happen in the event of a lawsuit or ordinance that resulted in people getting served. Anyway, the word 'telegram' was used. Telegram?!

That's how long it had been since those bylaws were examined thoroughly.

So, who's responsible? Well, the point is, we all are, if we have the privilege of a seat on the board. And here, as everywhere, relationships are key. Nonprofit leaders can absolutely empower their board members to be active participants in their organizations, and prioritizing relationships will help them do so. There are many ways to make this happen. For example, I've got a nonprofit-leader friend who swears by 'spreading the love,' adopting a horizontal approach to these relationships by encouraging every individual who sits on the board to liaise with a dedicated staff member.

GOVERNING THAT'S 'WITH' AND NOT 'FOR'

Social-movement-aligned funding networks, such as Resource Generation and Solidaire, are embracing alternative models of governance within their own organizations. These models reject top-down approaches, putting justice and equity front and center. In doing so, they aim to empower communities in their own decision-making.

I've already introduced you to the work of Resource Generation, and you can get a sense of its take on power by visiting the organization's website. Here's a taste: 'We believe social justice movements need to be led by communities most directly impacted by injustice. As young wealthy people, we support the leadership of working-class communities, poor people, communities of color, women, and LGBTQ folks in transformative social justice movements. We also bring our full selves and our own good thinking. We build cross-class relationships in working for a just healthy world.'

A look at how Solidaire describes its work is just as interesting: 'As a membership community of individual donors and foundation allies, Solidaire moves funding to progressive and radical movements with a commitment to building grassroots power in impacted communities. We also work together to transform philanthropic giving to create new relationships between donors and movements.'

In explaining how resources are organized (and money is moved) at Solidaire, the organization prioritizes work based on a number of principles. Among them is 'work that is led by people most directly impacted by injustice.' In this way, Solidaire seeks 'to challenge the traditional norms of the philanthropic sector' by working 'to influence the ways the philanthropic sector funds and builds relationships with movements and traditional funding streams.'

Whether these approaches appeal to you or not, I urge you to become familiar with them. Many of the younger donors I spoke with hold them in very high esteem, and as those donors develop and become influential in the sector, so too will organizations like these.

Whatever your protocols are for board performance, it's imperative that you actually follow them. At the risk of stating the obvious, ensuring that board members fulfill their obligations takes its own kind of commitment from nonprofit leaders. As a case in point, when I joined the board of the Girl Scouts, I was apprised of the organization's expectations. These expectations were a little intense, one of them being that every board member was required to bring in *another* board member, and to take that person through the process of qualification for board service. When I questioned the math – or how the Girl Scouts thought that each member of its twenty-five-member board could possibly bring in a new person, when the limit for membership was twenty-five – I got this in response, 'Lisa, nobody expects you to actually do that!'

So, here I was, a Girl Scout. I was trying to abide by the rules, as good Girl Scouts do. But it seemed to me the rules, or at least some of the rules, didn't mean anything. That's no way to govern. And while the action or manner of governing varies among nonprofits, follow-through is universal. Without it, none of this works.

As a final word, this also doesn't work unless boards engage collaboratively – with one other, with the staff and stakeholders of the organizations they represent, and even with other nonprofits. This takes trust, which is a happy result of good governance.

The other results? They're up to you.

HOW BOARDS HAVE CHANGED IN TWENTY-FIVE YEARS

Steven Windmueller is a noted American scholar and former Jewish communal professional. His perspective on the changing nature and function of boards reflects the depth of his knowledge about Jewish institutional trends, but what he's saying is applicable to the sector at large:

> Around twenty-five years ago, there was a shift in the responsibility and commitment to task that had previously been shared by board members and staff. In federations, synagogues, and national Jewish agencies, this involved a transfer of power to senior executives. The goal was that these organizations would be managed by their CEOs, with a corollary change in connection with the pay scale of these professionals – their salaries increased in comparison to other nonprofits. The shift was based on the notion that boards were too large, power was too dispersed, and competition within the Jewish nonprofit world was too

great. So, a more streamlined process based on a corporate business model was introduced, which has fundamentally changed the decision-making process.

'I wish I could trace for you the history of when boards started to become significant funding streams. Now, almost every board has introduced some version of a give or get mechanism. Historically, the idea was for the board to "represent" the community. Boards comprised a cross-section of individuals who brought to the table different sets of skills and knowledge concerning their roles as officers and board members. Those boards were, in fact, reflective of the community. Major donors were serving with individuals making minimalist gifts, and even non-donors, and together they were providing to these agencies fiduciary oversight and policy leadership.

'With the move to establish a corporate leadership model, we can identify a number of structural changes. As an example, executive directors became identified as presidents or CEOs. The corporate framework of these boards also changed.

'By way of background, I served on a local Jewish nonprofit board when the organization moved to adopt a corporate model involving give or get. In that first year, I diligently went out and asked folks to contribute to my quota, but was unsuccessful in reaching new and potential contributors. In hindsight, I can see that this agency has done exceptional work.

But the corporate model that they adopted didn't work for me.

Not all board members are the same! Folks come to board service with different strengths and, sadly, this particular model doesn't focus on drawing upon or emphasizing individualized skills.

'Issues surrounding how to treat donors have existed for a very long time, including the one driven by the belief that if donors know too much they might stop giving. I had a chat, for example, with an executive director of a synagogue about how she had uncovered problems related to the rabbi's discretionary fund. For her, the bottom line was that this fund wasn't being monitored, and when she brought the matter to the board's attention, she was told to shut up.'

The mismanagement of funds that Steven is referring to, and the board's unwillingness to discuss it, may be a product of the fact that the institution in question qualified for religious exemption from the reporting requirements of a Form 990. So perhaps someone thought that the mess could be kept under wraps. This is problematic for all the reasons I've previously explored, but it's also not unique to religious institutions.

Again, much of what Steven describes is actually applicable to the sector at large. In fact, when I checked in with Steven recently, he let me know that at the time of our initial interview for this book, the increase in pay he describes above was more narrowly limited to key Jewish institutions. Today that's no longer the case, as salary increases such as these are now applied across the board to high-profile nonprofit executives.

As for the potential for mismanagement of funds existing in any organization – well, I have a donor friend, as one non-religious example, who describes being involved with a charity whose financial health he began to worry about. When he joined the organization's board, he expected there to be conversations about the issue, which had showed itself in myriad ways (missed payroll being one, as well as a growing 'crisis' mindset and increasing reliance on big donations). And yet at board meetings, those discussions didn't happen. It wasn't until the CEO left that the board realized the extent of the organization's troubles. And the CEO? He was partly to blame, but he had the power he needed to keep the board in the dark, probably because he was afraid of the loss of an important board-driven funding stream.

What's heartening, however, is that despite the changing nature and function of boards, ethics still matter to the people on them. My donor friend's organization righted itself following the departure of its CEO. And the synagogue's 'silenced' executive director? According to Steven, 'She told them she couldn't manage a system that had major ethical challenges. And she's at another synagogue now, which is being managed in a more appropriate way.'

'TEAMWORK MAKES THE DREAM WORK'

Coined by international leadership expert John C. Maxwell, this little saying about teamwork is undeniably relevant to philanthropy, where trust and good governance are ultimately about public good.

In 2019, *The Chronicle of Philanthropy* reported on how Case Western Reserve University and the Cleveland Clinic bucked philanthropic convention by reaching across the City of Cleveland and collaborating to raise $275M for a joint community project.

Initially, Case Western had been fundraising for a $50M project, but, following a call in 2012 between its president and the CEO of the Cleveland Clinic, that $50M project turned into a transformative initiative worth $515M, elements of which are already up and running today. This is all the more impressive when you learn that, in the early days of the project, these two visionary leaders and their teams looked for examples of this kind of collaboration to learn from. Sadly, such examples didn't seem to exist. Undeterred, the institutions moved forward anyway, forging an extraordinarily successful medical partnership.

As an active donor and board member, I was shocked to read, in *The Chronicle of Philanthropy*, that fundraisers from the Cleveland Clinic and Case Western 'worked together to develop a list of the donors and prospects they had in common'. Actually, scratch that. I was elated to read of their sharing. Because the traditional thinking goes a little like this:

- Share our donors? Won't they be poached? We worked so hard to get them!
- Share our prospects? But *we* did the research! Why should we share it with other fundraisers?
- A bigger project? What if it fails?
- How will we deal with the pitch? We've finally found our secret sauce and created a pitch that works, so why would we share our methods with other fundraisers?
- Who gets the credit if we're successful? Will our contributions be minimized? And won't people think that we couldn't go it alone or build the projects we'd planned without help from another nonprofit?
- I'm still uncomfortable about the sharing-our-donors part. How will we fundraise in the future if *our* donors are in bed with our competitors?
- Did you really mean share our donors?!

Sound familiar? As a donor, I get it – I do – but I also have to say that fundraisers who feel they *own* me by virtue of my support for their organizations ... well, that's just offensive. Do fundraisers really think that donors aren't aware of nonprofits working in the same space as the ones they've chosen to support? Do they think that when donors get behind *one* organization, it's because they're too lazy to build relationships with that organization's competitors? For me, it doesn't matter how much money I give, or that my support of an organization is long-term and ongoing. Nobody owns me.

As for the pitch and its 'secret sauce,' don't sweat it. There's no getting a patent on a pitch. The fact is, what's special about your charity will always be thus, and ditto for you personally as fundraisers. The real 'secret sauce' is how you comport yourselves when delivering your pitch – ideally, with empathy, honesty, respect, and transparency.

Finally, a word of reassurance to those who avoid collaboration because they're worried that it will fail. Here, success is the likelier prospect, and all the more when you partner well. As for the issue of credit and the optics of actually *needing* a partner to achieve success: that's ridiculous. Practically every hour I encounter a product, program or system that exists because of collaboration.

Collaboration has long been a buzzword in business, where even traditionalists are after the results that it yields. Let's look to those results for inspiration. Because, by partnering together, nonprofit professionals and board members will not only widen the net, meeting new colleagues and building relationships, they'll also engage in knowledge-sharing, trading techniques and strategies while making the 'dream' work and achieving their goals. What could be better?

SEVEN

GOOD COMMUNICATION

The Real Work of
Relationships

Communications experts worth their salt will tell you that the most important thing you can do, after determining the goals and objectives of your communications, is to know your target audience. For fundraisers, that audience is donors.

'Always make the audience suffer as much as possible,' was Alfred Hitchcock's motto, and as anyone who's seen *The Birds* will attest, it worked like a charm. I'm sure it's nobody's intention to reprise that motto in the full-hearted world of fundraising. Still, a great many donors are uncomfortable with how the organizations they support are communicating with them, and 'uncomfortable' is putting it mildly.

As you're no doubt aware, more than 60% of one-time donors (some put it closer to 70%) fail to contribute to an organization a second time. If you're trying to generate funding in order to keep a nonprofit alive, that's terrifying. So, while this book's earlier chapters looked at connecting with prospects and asking for money, what we're going to explore in this chapter on communication is how to build relationships with existing donors.

Because here's what I know. These donors *want* to continue to love you. They even want to hear from you – just not always in the ways that you might think.

Retention, Retention, Retention

Despite their best efforts – all that time and money and marketing – charities still have to find replacements for more than 60% of their donors annually, and that's just to *maintain* their yearly levels of giving. In fact, the 2018 Association for Fundraising Professionals (AFP) Fundraising Effectiveness Survey Report notes that, 'Gains of 5.989 million in new and previously lapsed donors were offset by losses of 5.908 million in lapsed donors. This means that there was a growth of 81,023 donors, and every 100 donors gained in 2017 was offset by 99 lost donors through attrition.'

The AFP's 2019 report is even more alarming for the way it demonstrates a progressive decline in retention. It found that the overall retention rate (which reflects the percentage of all donors giving to the same organization in 2018 as they did in 2017) fell by almost two percentage points in a year to 45.5%. And the new donor retention rate (which reflects donors who made first-time gifts in 2017, and then gave again in 2018) dropped by four percentage points to 20.2%.

Given the evidence, it doesn't take a genius to realize that there's a problem and it's getting worse. Why?

WHY DONORS STOP GIVING

The biennial 2018 US Trust Study of High Net-Worth Philanthropy conducted in partnership with the Indiana University Lilly Family School of Philanthropy found that 28% of wealthy donors stopped giving to at least one organization in 2017 alone. The reasons cited include too-frequent solicitations from the nonprofit (41%); a belief that the organization was not effective or did not sufficiently communicate its effectiveness (16%); and being asked by the nonprofit for an amount the donor felt was inappropriate (9%).

Naturally, most fundraisers follow the money. They spend the bulk of their time on donors with the capacity to give in the range of $10K or more. Fundraising jobs depend on these donors and lately, so does philanthropy.

Let me submit as evidence the only reason for the rise (albeit, the small rise) in overall giving of late. This reason is an increase in foundation grants that were in the seven figures and higher. Unfortunately, however, everyone is now competing for these mammoth gifts and not everyone is going to be successful. What happens to the sector then?

Worst case, it tanks. That's why it's imperative that we stop heeding the advice, so prolific in fundraising, that 'cultivation' is for the big givers only. Time is finite, of course, and quarterly targets are real. But directing all of our resources (which, let's face it, are famously limited in fundraising) at one, rarefied group of supporters – well, it pretty much sacrifices everyone else. At least on the level of relationships.

There are loads of ways of providing regular donors with the connection they crave – communications tactics, for example, that can help to align them with your organization's mission or keep them abreast of its successes without making them feel like they're always a 'mark.' Knowing your donors will help you deploy these tactics, which aren't nearly as crass as they sound and also don't always require a major reallocation of resources.

But before we get super-prescriptive, let's take a look at why retention is so important to an organization's bottom line. Jay Love, who serves on the board of the Center of Philanthropy at Indiana University, has some interesting things to say about the matter on Bloomerang, the blog he co-founded in 2012. I'll paraphrase:

- *Most major gifts are made after five years of giving.* Very few big gifts represent first, second or even third donations to a charity. Four to five years of relationship development with a donor who subsequently comes forward with a major gift is much more common, which is enough to give retention new meaning. Add to this timeline the fact that a single, six-figure gift can equal more, for many charities, than all the other gifts from that year's newly acquired donors and, again, retention really becomes something to strive for.

- *Lifetime value is real.* This is the total amount contributed to a charity over a donor's lifetime and it really adds up – sometimes to the tune of thousands of dollars, even for the smallest direct-mail donors. What it means organizationally is that spending extra time (for example, by reallocating a staff member) to build relationships with your donors, regardless of their dollar value, will really pay off in the long term, boosting not only retention, but your bottom line.
- *It's more expensive to acquire new donors than it is to retain existing ones.* Continually acquiring new donors can easily cost an organization 50 to 100% more than what those donors actually give, in terms of dollar amounts.

Convinced yet? Even more persuasive is the fact that it's often several years before any nonprofit will break even (in terms of dollars raised versus dollars spent) in their efforts to acquire new donors. So again, investing in your existing base – really doing what it takes to make folks want to stick around – is frankly just good business.

The Very Real Problem of Donor Fatigue

Let's say you're an organization that only *really* cultivates your biggest donors. Does this mean you ignore your supporters whose gifts are more moderate?

In my experience, organizations actually do the opposite. Regular donors are often overwhelmed with communication from the nonprofits they support – especially on Giving Tuesday or at the end of the year; sometimes even *all* year – and much of this communication is impersonal. It doesn't reflect the fact that the donors are known in any way by the organizations they support, or that their giving history and habits are known. On the contrary, now that these donors' names are on the mailing lists of organizations they've contributed to, they often get sent stuff (mass solicitations, for example) indiscriminately.

Asking for money again and again won't increase your chances of getting it, and nor will it encourage loyalty from the donors you want to retain. So why am I compelled to repeat, in this section on fatigue, the most overused cliché of all time? You probably know it – it's the one about doing the same thing over and over and still expecting a different result.

Nonprofits, I'm looking at you.

There is something very misguided about the thinking that governs nonprofit dealings with regular (or recurring) donors; namely, the belief that donors should 'give until it hurts and then give a bit more.' We discussed this approach in Chapter Two.

And sure, it probably started with democratic intentions – the idea, for example, that for a $10 donor, giving an extra $5 may hurt; while for others, that 'punishing' additional amount might look more like $100, $1000 or $100,000. Still, it's a little insulting. And over the long term, especially among donors whose continued support of a cause *already* reflects their commitment to it – well, it can actually start to feel like harassment.

It goes without saying that nonprofits face rising costs, the pressure to compete by expanding on their programs or creating new ones, and increasing fears that only the very wealthy will support charities in the future.

Once any donor is engaged with your organization, you naturally want them to be *more* engaged. You want them to give more. But here's where the math doesn't make sense to me. If so many donors are dropping off after the first donation, shouldn't we look beyond the stats to understand why? Then, shouldn't we change our behavior to ensure that we're not, as the old adage goes, 'doing the same thing over and over and expecting a different result?'

Here's a typical me-and-my-charity relationship arc:

- I engage with an organization that's new to me by donating a modest amount. I'm happy about it! I make a real effort to learn more about the organization and to deepen my relationship with it, almost always to the extent that I start to feel invested and aligned with its mission.
- Somewhere between months three and twelve post-donation, I'm asked to increase my gift. Frequently, I'm

even asked to increase my *annual* gift. But not once have we had a discussion about my gift being annual! The old me might have given more at this point (I was pretty naive), but these days I'm far more likely to just tell the fundraiser that I never intended for my gift to be annual. I'll tell her straight-out that I'm only willing to give what I gave last year. Then (and here's what should be concerning to you) I'll trust her a little bit less going forward.

- There's still a scenario in which I might give more after being asked to increase my gift, but only if I really love the organization and feel good about how it's run, what it's doing, and how it has handled the ask for more money. (Remember, our relationship at this point spans three to twelve months.) In fact, I will *often* give more in this scenario, and that's a lesson too.

- If I *do* give more, and then am asked *again* to increase my already-increased gift – well, that's when I start to think that I've been had. I may suspect that the 'respectful' relationship I believed we were building was just a ruse. I may even find myself apologizing for the 'inadequate' size of my gift. Do I feel good about apologizing? No. Do I continue to do it when approached in this way? Yes. A part of that is on me. But what my apologies also speak to is the fact, frankly, that I'm being manipulated.

And so it goes. I actually had a terrible epiphany the other day about how easy it would be to avoid these scenarios, or at least the worst of them, by limiting my giving to the wholly sporadic.

If I were to give off and on, for example, I'd be immune to the assumptions fundraisers often make about recurring donors. Organizations would court me and thank me – first gifts are much more likely to be appropriately acknowledged – and then, after I ignored their subsequent advances, they'd let go of the idea that, as a 'regular' donor, I owe them. They'd finally leave me alone. After skipping a year or two, I could even start the process all over again with the same organization and be thanked as if I were a brand-new donor.

But do I really want to play that game? No. Nobody wants that, me included.

Today's always-on culture has made information overload a thing with which most of us are all too familiar, whatever the context. Add to this verbal clutter daily emails from multiple nonprofits, many of which communicate a situation of 'crisis.' Now imagine that you are in a position to mitigate this crisis – because when you're the donor receiving these emails, you understand that this is what they're communicating, too.

PRE-EMPTING DISASTER FATIGUE

The 2019 report from Barclays, 'Barriers to Giving: Research into the evolving world of philanthropy,' highlights the positive influence of social media in driving awareness of global events. As the report states, 'Anger, outrage and sorrow expressed in relation to tragic world events can lead discussion and debate when they go viral on social media channels, prompting potential wealthy donors to consider how they can help.'

The report also identifies a downside: 'Another trend recognized by charities, experts and intermediaries is that individuals are focusing on giving to an end cause, rather than an organization or charity itself.'

Already, organizations are taking steps to address this trend. A 2019 *Chronicle of Philanthropy* article, 'Worried About More Than a Possible Recession,' describes how staff at Habitat for Humanity – concerned that donors who give to one disaster after another might eventually become fatigued and stop giving – created a major disaster preparedness program, called Habitat Strong. The program aims to minimize the impact of natural disasters by creating dwellings that can withstand them. It's been hugely successful and represents a 'pivot' of the sort that happens in for-profit business all the time.

Some organizations send me email every day. I also receive snail mail and phone calls and text messages from charities, but let's set these aside for the time being and ask ourselves this: who, in their right mind, wants this level of crisis-laden contact? I welcome such frequency from Word of the Day (which emails me uncommon words, along with their definitions, pronunciations, and origins, daily). But that's because I signed up for it – I *volunteered* to expand my vocabulary. So, while the experts in content marketing or brand building might urge you to ignore my advice and keep at it, I'm going to ask that you think differently.

Here's why. The 'unsubscribe' button is within everyone's reach. And even if donors don't act on how insulted I *guarantee* you they feel by such an obviously impersonal and relentless approach, they're probably going to just push that button and be done with you.

In nonprofits, there's a direct link between this approach, which is frankly just unproductive, and poorly parsed lists. It's enough to say for now that I may be perfectly comfortable telling an organization, 'Sorry, this isn't my thing.' But I'd like to avoid having to 'let down' (over and over and over again) those organizations I already support. And I'd *definitely* like to avoid feeling like my only option is to cut ties with an organization, or even to announce, as I have in the past, 'I need a break from all the pitches. Please call me in a few months.'

My friend Jeremy has decided that when fundraisers come calling in the future, his response is going to go something like this: 'Look, thanks for getting in touch, but the only cause I support is Diabetes. When we find a cure for Diabetes, I'll be happy to donate to your charity. Until then, please take me off your lists.'

Of course, Jeremy is describing pitch situations in which he's a prospective donor, as opposed to a recurring one. But the fact that he thinks this way – and is willing to go to such imaginative lengths with nonprofits – speaks volumes.

Fundraisers: put yourself in a donor's shoes.

Let's use me as an example. Right now, I'm sitting in my office. Just about every available surface is covered in little signs made out of cardstock – signs on which I've recorded some of the stats you see in this book. On the wall next to the window leading out to the garden hangs my Girl Scouts sash, which I've framed, and it's pretty much covered in badges. When I turn to the computer and open your email, this is what's going through my head: I'm an avid reader and I want to do good. I also want to fall in love with the organizations I support. So I do feel compelled, especially as a donor, to carefully and responsibly read everything.

The email I got from you is one of dozens just like it, most of which have totally generic subject lines and a ton of verbal clutter. Do I read or do I *not* read?

These days, it's mostly the latter. And while this might sound strange, when I'm scanning my inbox – today, I counted twenty solicitations before 9:30 a.m. – I sometimes think of the musical *Hamilton*. It's a favorite in our house and even in my car, where the twins will put the soundtrack on the stereo and recite it all verbatim. In these moments, it's impossible not to be impressed by Lin-Manuel Miranda's attention to every single word that he wrote – a high bar to set for nonprofits, I realize, but why not? Sometimes, even a small change can affect how your communication resonates. It's the same with a change in perspective. If *you* were to get the email you're writing, would its subject line compel you to open it? Would you read it right to the end?

BRINGING 'PLAIN LANGUAGE' TO NONPROFIT COMMUNICATIONS

Did you know that 'plain language' is actually a movement? I'm not kidding. Conventions haven't changed much when it comes to good writing, but our attention spans have diminished – and no wonder. Here are a few gems applicable to all your communications from the US Government's interpretation of plain language principles:

- Less is more! Be concise
- Be clear! Organize your thoughts in a way that serves your reader's needs
- Use headings often and make sure they're useful (consider where your readers' eyes go naturally, for example, and lead them from point to point with headings)
- Remember that questions often make great headings
- Use 'you' to speak to the reader
- Use the active voice
- Use short sections and shorter sentences
- Make liberal use of white space so your pages are easy to scan
- Eliminate unnecessary words

Donor Fatigue, Multiplied

I had an interesting conversation on Twitter recently about different perspectives on end-of-year fundraising. I had added my voice (or tweets) to a growing chorus of donors who were upset about the lack of timely thanks from charities during the crazy final week of the year. My own rant had a dual focus. First, I was annoyed by the fact that I hadn't been thanked for contributions I'd made during the last week of December this past year. And second, I couldn't believe that I was still getting emails from organizations to which I'd *just* contributed – emails informing me that it was my 'last chance to give!'

The issue of thanks is something I will tackle in this book's final chapter. But do know, for now, that I'm not expecting the world. Even an autoreply confirming my donation (and thanking me for it) would have been absolutely fine if it also meant that I wouldn't immediately be asked to give again to the very same organization.

Because, come on!

As for that Twitter conversation, it turns out I'm not the only donor out there who feels frustrated at the end of the year, and nor am I the only donor interested in finding solutions that work. And by 'work,' I mean for *everyone* involved in donor solicitation and retention. The knee-jerk 'fundraising is a really hard job' response is not, unfortunately, among these solutions.

Fundraising *is* a really hard job. So, isn't it in everyone's interest to ensure that it not get harder? Because this is a likely reality, what with retention numbers on the downtick and finance, communications, technology, and the demographics of donors changing so rapidly. And sure, there are many organizations that have embraced these changes. They've found innovative ways to manage the delicate balance, still so necessary in philanthropy, of old world and new. It's probably to these organizations that I owe my thanks for this year's drop in Giving Tuesday emails.

But consider this: I still received more emails than I could ever possibly read. In the past, my Giving Tuesday total has hovered at around 200, give or take. This year, I received around 100 emails, and I also didn't get any solicitations over the phone. Which is a relief, of course, since I'd been mentally preparing for the Giving Tuesday onslaught for the two weeks before it began.

And don't get me wrong, the thinking behind Giving Tuesday – that is, the identification (and orchestration) of a global day of generosity – is noble and smart. It started in 2012, when New York City's 92nd Street Y partnered with the UN Foundation to try to counteract some of the crazy materialism of Thanksgiving weekend's Black Friday and Cyber Monday. Fast forward to 2019, when Giving Tuesday raised a staggering $500M in the US alone, a 25% increase from the year previous that reflects an average donation of between $100 and $140.

That's pretty amazing.

Not so amazing, unfortunately, is the way the day plays out. For a 'movement' that claims to be about doing good in any way you can (per the Giving Tuesday website, 'giving and volunteering') I don't see a lot of giving of much of anything other than money. Most of the 'beyond cash' examples that I uncovered after a little digging were anecdotal. And, not one of the 100 emails I received said a word about non-cash donations.

GIVING TUESDAY AWARDS

I love when organizations use Giving Tuesday as an opportunity to craft emails that are clear, creative, and fun. Here are some of my favorites from this year's season:

- The many organizations that used their all-important subject-line 'real estate' to announce matching Giving Tuesday donations (for example, 'Invest in Clean Water This Giving Tuesday! Donations Matched!'). Even for existing donors who aren't particularly keen on being solicited by organizations they already support, the prospect of a matching donation (which leverages your gift) is intriguing.

- Any organization that included a subject-line message detailing, in as few words as possible, what a Giving Tuesday donation would accomplish. Among the best I saw was, 'This Giving Tuesday, Invest in a Tipping Point for Peace' (Alliance for Middle East Peace). And, 'Invest in Diverse Reporting this Giving Tuesday' (International Women's Media Foundation). And, 'This Giving Tuesday, Save Animals' (Los Angeles Zoo). I've been a supporter of most of these organizations in the past, and I was reminded this year (by a subject line, no less!) of exactly what they manage to get right.

Then there are the emails that *didn't* impress. Here's a sampling:

- The many, many nonprofits who delivered subject line fails such as, 'It's here!' And, 'It's Giving Tuesday!' And, 'What's Going on Today!' And, 'Today is Giving Tuesday. You Can Make a Difference!' Fundraisers, this is a movement. Donors are getting these emails in the hundreds. Please give us a reason to want to read them.
- Any organization that decided to start soliciting in advance. Subject-line examples in this camp include, 'We need you Tomorrow!' And, 'Tomorrow's the Day!' And, 'Giving Tuesday is less than 48 hours away!'
- The one misguided organization that sent me a calendar entry invite in the subject line of a Giving Tuesday email. Granted, I calendar lots of things – birthday reminders, dentist appointments, charity-event ticket deadlines – but I'm not ever going to log a prompt for Giving Tuesday.

The movement is also challenging from a business perspective. Many charities participate in Giving Tuesday because, in a way, they can't *not*. So, they throw minimal resources at it by glomming on, so to speak, to the bandwagon: setting up a dedicated webpage and then sending out a bunch of emails. But as per the idea of this being a 'movement,' these are *mass* emails. Which brings me back to the experience of recurring donors.

What does it look like at the existing donor's end? This group already has a relationship with the charities that are soliciting them on Giving Tuesday. If they're frequent givers, they're dealing with volume – lots of emails from lots of charities, including those that they don't support financially. They're probably stressed as a result, and maybe even questioning their year-end giving.

Here are the questions that come up for me:

- *Why don't organizations parse their lists?* Were they to do so, they could let their existing donors off the hook on Giving Tuesday. Even better, they could heed the advice that's been circulating lately and use the day to thank their regular donors while continuing to solicit new ones.
- *Is the message here that I don't give enough?* Because if I give money to an organization during the year, and then I get pushy solicitations from that organization on Giving Tuesday, it really begs the question.
- *Do donors really give on the fifth email, if they chose not to give on the second?* When I see an organization that I'm familiar with but have yet to support, an organization that

sends me three or four or *five* emails between the Sunday before Giving Tuesday and Giving Tuesday itself, I'm highly likely to scratch it off the list I keep, which tracks potential recipients of my money. For better or for worse, that organization has ruined its relationship with me forever.

- *Does a charity's lack of professionalism on Giving Tuesday reflect larger organizational problems?* Like direct mail, Giving Tuesday tends to bring in donations with a lower dollar value. As a result, it can be one of those 'what the heck – we have nothing to lose!' projects for charities, something assigned to junior staff and/or not really afforded much thought. But if you offend me on Giving Tuesday by being too pushy with email or using hastily put-together messaging, you risk losing my trust in your brand.

Not to pile on, but we're talking about the end of the year – the busiest time of the fundraising cycle. I'd accept this, if end-of-year donor fatigue made us give more. If it were just the necessary by-product of a functioning system, I'd brace myself for the onslaught, and move on. But the research clearly shows that the sector's problems with retention are a direct result of over-solicitation and ignoring this helps no one.

MY YEAR-END NONPROFIT
COMMUNICATIONS TALLY

Year-end snail mail. It makes me sad to think of the money wasted and the landfill impacted by the hundreds of envelopes I get – mainly from organizations that I've never supported and am unlikely to support in the future. The response rates on snail-mail solicitations (especially the ones in letter-sized envelopes stamped with a pre-printed name and barcode) are in steady decline, and while snail mail is certainly appropriate for donors who have identified it as preference, most of us would rather see you spend your money elsewhere. That said, if you insist on using snail mail to send, for example, a beautiful invitation, *do* also send a format-appropriate digital equivalent.

Year-end email solicitations. I've already gone on about these at length. Just know this: if a world event occurs in the fourth quarter that requires a special fundraising effort for an un-budgeted need, I will welcome your email. Otherwise, I'm busy getting gifts out to friends and family and trying to find a moment, most importantly, to enjoy some holiday time with my husband and kids.

Year-end text messages. Texts are great, in fundraising, for reminders and notifications about legitimate last-minute needs or membership renewals. But at the end of the year, those texts are just annoying. Like a lot of people, I'm also getting texts from friends and family – they're what I want and need to prioritize now.

Development people: I understand that you work extraordinarily hard, and that this seasonal push brings in a significant amount of money for your organizations. Which, of course, is the point, because those charitable dollars fuel meaningful outcomes in philanthropy. But I also know that the timing of the push dovetails with your year-end targets. Many donors don't share the urgency you express leading up to December 31st. Furthermore, as tax laws change (see pages 142–3) and non-time-sensitive Donor Advised Funds grow in popularity, your year-end fundraising 'emergency' will align even less with the giving habits of your supporters.

So, with an eye to addressing donor fatigue, particularly the fatigue of the fourth quarter, and increasing retention, why not consider dedicating a resource to fundraising in March? Or for that matter, July? The results might surprise you.

Also, shine a light on those lists. They're your first step in personalizing communications. And, yes, the practice of list-parsing takes discipline, not to mention additional resources, at least during initial set-up. But as database technology evolves and becomes more accessible to nonprofits, is there any excuse not to embrace it?

Besides, if handled with care, the lists that form your

database can both power your fundraising and empower your supporters. Donors who *should* be left alone (maybe because they *just* gave you $500) can be graciously thanked and, yes, left alone. Likewise, donors who need a check-in can be afforded that courtesy via email (if that's what they prefer) or whatever represents their communications vehicle of choice. You may disagree, but whether they give, or they don't give, in this example, is not the point. For now (and hopefully forever) they're still supporters.

COMMON COMMUNICATIONS TRAPS AND WHAT THEY NET

Action	Reaction
Thrice-weekly emails from the same organization.	I stop reading emails from the organization and get annoyed.
Any piece of communication I receive from an organization with which I have a relationship that comes via a channel other than the one I typically use.	Either you know (and are ignoring) how I prefer to receive communications from your organization, or you haven't bothered to ask. In each case, I feel disrespected.

Any piece of communication with the words, 'Donate now!' Or, 'Before it's too late!'	I worry that the situation at the organization sending the email is as dire as the email suggests. Then, I wonder why I should give again. Clearly, my initial gift made little difference.
Any piece of communication asking me to give a smaller amount 'today!' than the amount I gave recently.	Since you appear not to be capable of parsing your lists, I start to wonder how professionally your organization is run.
Seemingly arbitrary phone calls and/or voicemail from organizations I don't personally know.	I'm suspicious of unscheduled phone calls and am far more likely to respond to an email with detailed information.
Ads or canned copy at the bottom of every email, with stock directive such as 'Join us now!'	Hasn't everyone on your recipient list *already* joined? Have I been sent this email in error?
An ask in every email.	You're making it very clear that I'm nothing more than a dollar sign, and every aspect of the message now reads like a 'hook.' It's not necessary to make an ask in every communication.

'It's Giving Tuesday!' **Or, 'It's December 31st!'**	I know what I day it is, and I'm already overwhelmed. Please give me a reason to keep reading.

Strategy: It's Bigger Than You Think

Communication is strategic when it advances an organization's mission, vision, and values, as well as its business goals. People often get too granular with this stuff, confusing what it means to be tactical (which is much more about the tools and channels you choose to communicate with, or the types of content you create) with being strategic. The great and important thing about communications strategy is that it's 'big picture.' It can drive and unify everything you want to say about your organization, and all the different ways you want to say it.

Did I mention big picture? We don't engage it enough in our thinking. We don't consider strategy. This is mostly because we spend a whole lot of time in the 'weeds' of deadlines and targets and lists – everything that's necessary to keep the lights on and the money flowing to our beneficiaries.

I'd like to re-introduce you to Felice Mancini. You may remember her from Chapter Two's conversation about motives. Here, Felice discusses how her thinking has evolved during the many years she's served as executive director of the Mr. Holland's Opus Foundation (MHOF) – which, among other things, gets musical instruments to underprivileged kids.

When I started at the foundation, I really didn't connect with music education. I connected with music. But the more I learned over the years about music education and what it means to people, especially children, the more I realized what the broader implications were of this sort of education – or really just of music – the more the work became, for me, about a kid's future. The kids we work with are from low-income families, and these kinds of things tend to affect them to a greater degree than their more advantaged peers.

So, the case I'm making to donors and supporters now is that this is much bigger than music education. It really is a youth development piece. It's about steering a life. That's exciting to me. And because an instrument is visual and tactile, it's also easy for people to relate to. People can actually visualize the moment that we put an instrument into the hands of a child.

I would hazard a guess that Felice's big-picture moment – her realization that the work of the foundation was about 'steering a life' – changed everything. It became part of the strategic case she made to donors, and it's probably now a theme in her communications and outreach.

My development-director friend Margot might call Felice lucky in that she's not part of the 'revolving door' of fundraising. Margot says, 'There are a few people out there who have worked for their organizations forever. These holdouts are unlike the vast majority of fundraisers who tend to move on within eighteen months, and it's much easier for them to ask for money. It takes a good year to know your job and even longer, sometimes, to understand the mission and vision of your organization and be able to talk about it.'

CONNECTING WITH EXISTING DONORS

The usual way	How it's received	How to do better
You made your annual commitment at around this time last year. Would you please send us your annual gift?	What annual gift? We haven't had that conversation.	Let's talk and review how your goals have evolved and how we can be a part of your giving going forward.
You gave $5,000 last year. This year, can you swing $10,000?	Exactly when will you be satisfied with my support?	Let's talk and review how your goals have evolved and how we can be a part of your giving going forward.
We want to be among the top three organizations that you support.	Why is it necessary for me to choose three?	How does our organization fit into the larger context of your giving?
We're asking you to give until it hurts, and then give a bit more.	Why would you want me to hurt myself?	We appreciate that you give in a meaningful way.

We're aware that you've already given this year, but this is a different campaign. Will you give again?	Exactly when will you be satisfied with my support?	We have a new initiative that feels like a good match for you. Absolutely no pressure. If you're interested, I'm happy to get you more information.
Lunch ... fawn ... socialize ... fawn. And then the requisite, 'Before you go ...' followed by a pitch.	I will never get back these two hours.	Let me know in advance that our meeting will involve an ask. At the meeting, engage in friendly conversation, but please don't fawn. Introduce your new initiatives and ask for my support.
We really need to win this election. Please send $5,000 by midnight.	The election is months away. What exactly is so urgent?	We so appreciate you supporting this campaign. A gift of $5,000 right now will provide 200 additional hours of canvassing, which we think will get us across the finish line.

We'd love to catch up and get your thoughts on our new initiative.	My thoughts or my money?	We'd love to see if you have interest in supporting an initiative we're launching or can connect us to people who might.
I'd love to get together to see how you're doing.	Is this a pitch or do you actually care about me?	I'd love to get together to see how you're doing. I promise, no pitches.
There's a thought leader in town, whom we think you'd like to meet. We're having a small gathering.	I'd love to hear that thought leader speak, but the gathering will end with a pitch.	We appreciate your past support and think you might enjoy meeting this thought leader. We're having a small gathering that won't include a pitch.
I realize that you told me 'no' last month. What about this month?	What does the word 'no' mean to you?	I respect your giving priorities and I won't ask you again until next year.

Let's have lunch. Our development director will be joining us.	Can't we get together to talk about the organization without a babysitter present?	We want to give you an update on our work. Would you like to schedule a call or a meeting with our director of development?

In theory, effective strategic communications planning should make it a million times easier for even new staff to align themselves *and* their donors with their organizations' core objectives. But it's a big topic, even among communications professionals, and I don't want to shift from our focus on fundraising. Instead, I'm going isolate the one aspect of communications strategy to which everyone can relate.

Storytelling: Because It's How We Connect Anyway

Storytelling is having a bit of a moment in today's workplace, and no wonder. Anybody with experience in sales will tell you that you've got to repeat the same message over and over again until you draw people in – that's what's going to make you successful. As Felice Mancini has learned, stories enable us to do this naturally. And, people pay attention! The desire to tell and be told stories is one of the most basic elements of human culture.

As fundraisers, when you choose storytelling as a means of engagement, via the careful use of words, images or video, your donors are much more likely to invest emotionally, not only in your cause and your organization, but also in *themselves* as a part of the solution.

A good story also has 'legs' and can help to ensure that your donors are your best ambassadors. While they may not remember the particulars of your charity's mission statement or your fundraising campaign's key messages, donors *will* internalize your story and – if it's especially compelling – they'll tell it to their friends.

Why? Because stories connect and inspire us. And since the best stories usually center around a hero – someone who faces a challenge, gets help from others, and beats the odds – they mimic what we do in philanthropy. That's powerful, and we need to use it to our advantage.

Felice talks about the fact that donors still come to the MHOF after having seen the film *Mr. Holland's Opus*, which was originally released in 1995. Evidently, these donors want to support the MHOF after being moved by the plight of the fictional students of Kennedy High, whose music program is threatened on account of budget cuts introduced in the film by the Board of Education. Donors also come to Felice after being inspired by Glenn Holland (the character played by Richard Dreyfus) and what he accomplished at Kennedy High through music.

Such an enduring link to great Hollywood storytelling is not the norm among charities, I get that. These days, though, there exists a ton of information on the Internet and elsewhere that's specific to narrative strategy. This information details how organizations can use their unique stories to better connect with their stakeholders. The beauty of it is that even smaller organizations (those without a dedicated communications team, for example) can take steps toward leveraging narrative. As I've said, our sector in particular is *full* of raw material, we just need to put it to use.

To that end, what do our stories – especially in donor outreach – actually look like in practice? Writing recently in the *Chronicle of Philanthropy*, public relations and corporate responsibility specialist Maura F. Farrell has some useful advice, the gist of which highlights how purposeful we can be in the way we tell our stories and connect with donors because we've got so many ways to communicate.

For example, Maura has this to say about social media: '[It] can be a huge boon to your nonprofit; after all, it enables you to interact with your audiences in real time. You do not need to rely on others to tell your stories. You can see exactly what captivates donors.'

USING SOCIAL MEDIA TO KEEP
DONORS ENGAGED

Writing in the *Chronicle of Philanthropy*, public relations expert Maura F. Farrell advises nonprofits to enlist social media to keep donors engaged. Here are some of her main points in brief:

- If your resources are slim or you find all the platforms overwhelming, pick the channels that matter most to your supporters. These days, our ability to track user behavior on social media makes this easy to do.
- Pay attention to what's trending on any given day and see if there's a way to connect it to the work of your organization. Not only will this highlight your relevance, it might also win you new supporters.
- Include pictures or video. Messages with images are 40 times more likely to get shared on social media than those without.
- Be consistent. If you start strong and then become less active over time, you'll lose your audience.

What captivates donors is obviously important to any exploration of nonprofit communications and outreach. I wholeheartedly agree with Maura's suggestion that fundraisers ask donors how they like to receive their communications and also which stories resonate. Social media is incredibly useful in this regard, since it lets us easily track user visits as well as 'likes' and 'shares.'

But all our communications channels can be thoughtful deliverers of story. Being selective about what you tell, how and why you tell it, and to whom – that's what matters. If you do that, then you're very likely to get my attention. As a donor, I may even be willing to share your success story with my own networks through email, social media, and good old word of mouth.

GETTING GRAPHIC WITH YOUR STANDARDS

Writing in the blog 'Classy: Online Fundraising for the Modern Nonprofit,' marketing strategy expert Pam Georgina recommends that all nonprofits develop 'brand books' in order to professionalize and advance their communications materials. 'Nonprofits need to promote a positive brand identity,' Pam insists, 'and maintain consistency across marketing channels and platforms in order to build trust and confidence for their mission. Without this, it can be difficult to build deep relationships and sustain long-term loyalty.'

A brand book is a compendium of conventions and tips, basically the equivalent of a text-focused editorial 'style guide.' Both guidebooks are specific to the way an organization tells its story, whether visually or textually, and both are common practice in business. The idea is that they bring staff on board, ensuring that their communications always capture (and stay true to) the 'feel' of their organization's mission, vision, and values. They also save time by creating a template of sorts for mailings, invites, and so on. At minimum, Pam recommends that the contents of a brand book include guidelines for logos, approved fonts, and when they should be used, specific brand colors, and image guidelines.

Your donors have stories too. Josh once told his story in an incredibly emotional video that was part of the Cedars-Sinai Medical Center's 'Grateful Patient' series. The video was shown at one of the Cedars' annual meetings, and the feeling in the room was that rather than being manipulative, which is sometimes a fear, the video honored everyone. Josh too! It not only held our attention, it justified all of our reasons for being involved.

Also, stories aren't just vehicles for 'soft' information. They can provide a meaningful framework for the communication of all the facts and figures and metrics that are part of your reporting obligations to donors. They allow people to 'experience' information that might otherwise be boring. And they acknowledge the fact that hey, maybe a donor is done giving money in the immediate, but that doesn't mean he isn't still interested in the programs he helped to support or what's new with the organization in general.

ANNUAL REPORTS AND THE QUESTION
OF PRINT

Annual reports are a bit of a lightning rod in any conversation about print versus digital. Although people have been talking about their demise for years, they persist – sometimes costing the organizations that produce them thousands upon thousands of dollars. I don't *love* annual reports (I happen to think that few people read them) and I definitely recommend that you do a readership survey to determine whether they should still play a role in your communications strategy.

Also, these sorts of products (assuming they're print) must come with digital companions. Annual reports are responsibility-focused pieces of communication – they fulfill an organization's reporting obligations for the fiscal year – and as such, they have to be accessible, which these days means digital. The case for print still exists, but it might be time to move away (or at least *consider* moving away) from that perfect-bound fifty-page opus.

Thinking about communications from a storytelling perspective encourages a 'human' approach to philanthropic relationships. It also asks us to be *just that little bit* more creative, which is vital in the world of under-resourced nonprofits. For

253

example, emailing a donor with a little anecdote about a person who benefited from the program she supports, making it personal – that's taking a step toward ensuring that you're not just relating to your donors by rote.

An acquaintance of mine runs a huge nonprofit whose focus is social advocacy. He says, 'Donors want to feel that their relationships with you aren't about money. That's why we have stewards, people who can interact with donors and figure out what they need. And with our younger clientele especially, they don't necessarily *need* a predetermined "donor experience."

'The interesting thing that happens is that people open up when you treat them like individuals. They're able to tell us what aspects of the organization they care about, and this enables us to have "normal" relationships with them.'

The Part About Knowing Your Audience

How do we get to know anyone? Proximity is usually a factor (though not always with donors and fundraisers) and so is curiosity and time. I'd therefore recommend that you get curious with your donors. Ask them what they're about and what their preferences are – for newsy communications, solicitations, face-to-face contact, and more.

My fundraiser friend Sheila says it best. 'Think about dating,' she suggests. 'What if donors and fundraisers knew – just like you know when you're dating – that they'll have a period of getting to know each other and then they'll have "the talk."

They'll talk about their dreams and expectations for the future and figure out together if something is there. Do they believe in marriage? Do they want to have kids? People ask these questions early on when they're dating, and their equivalents exist in fundraising.

'As a development director, I'd love to know that my donors and I will continue to be curious over time. Is there still purpose to our check-ins, and to the investment that we're making in each other? Do we still believe it serves the cause? I'd personally feel better if I knew that I was in a mutually respectful, committed relationship with someone whose commitment might mean a gift in the future.'

I can tell you, as a donor, that I'd feel better in this scenario too.

But everyone is different, and that's the point. Here's what Resource Generation's Andrea Pien told me: 'When I make a grant, I try to make it multi-year. Someone from the receiving organization will say, "What do we need to do in order to guarantee this multi-year grant?" But my feeling is that if I researched the organization, I trust them. I know that they'll do good stuff with the money, and I don't want them to get bogged down in pleasing me. So, I'll tell them to keep doing what they're doing; don't land in the news; send the annual reports you usually send; and, if it's convenient, we'll do a visit sometime. That's what I want my collaboration with nonprofits to look like.'

Many donors from Andrea's generation expressed to me their preference for mobilizing other people's money as a way of deepening their relationships with the organizations they support. Some of these donors might eventually opt for a more participatory expression of their philanthropy by 'leaving' traditional organizations and forming group-investment giving circles of their own.

Then again, we all come to a cause for a reason. In fact, I'll go out on a limb here and say that any regular donor thinking of leaving a charity is just as likely to stay.

So, be professional, where professionalism is warranted. But don't ever forget the heart in this work. Donors and fundraisers can enhance – or squander – the human touch in each and every communication.

IF THERE WERE A HOLY GRAIL OF FUNDRAISING

Recurring revenue has been a big thing in business for years, but does it hold the same prestige in fundraising?

It should. Donors who invite charities to monthly bill their credit cards tend *not* to disinvite them. Unless you're me, of course – which is a story that nicely rounds out this chapter.

A couple of years ago, I started a recurring monthly donation program at one of my alma maters. As is my habit in these giving scenarios, I happily let it continue. Then I left my credit card in a movie theater. I received a new one in the mail a couple of days later – a card just like the original, but for the last few numbers. I updated these numbers where I could and otherwise waited, assuming (as you do) that any vendor who needed me would quickly get in touch.

Shortly thereafter, a representative from the alma mater that hosted my recurring donation program (a large university) contacted me via email. I was told, tersely, that my card had been declined and my name removed from their database. A link to the donor website was included in the email, but the link took me to a generic giving page that didn't allow me to update my card. Instead, it sent me to a solicitation page where I was encouraged to become (again!) a recurring donor. Basically, I was persona non grata.

Why?

Obviously, recurring donations aren't big-ticket gifts. These things will never put a name on a building. But does that justify the lack of thanks they get, which is often the case after month three?

Consider this:

- Recurring monthly donors give 440% more to a charity over their lifetime than one-time donors.
- 52% of Millennials are more likely to give a monthly donation versus a one-time donation.
- Monthly supporters *continue* to donate to an organization for much longer than other donors. After one year, 80% of monthly donors continue their giving. After five years, 95% continue.

See the beauty? Now add to these benefits this little fact about monthly donors: they're typically just doing their thing during the madness of the fourth quarter, and so their money continues to come in. You can allocate your resources elsewhere. Also, these donors are giving you a fixed amount of cash, over and over again; they enable you to plan. And, many of them are Millennials!

Let's give these programs (and donors) the props they deserve. The longevity of philanthropy depends on it.

EIGHT

EVENTS FOR A NEW ERA

*Because We All Want
Something More Meaningful*

When I joined the Cedars' Board of Governors, my development liaison presented me with a list of fancy events we were now eligible to attend. But I had to be honest with her: I hate gala events. They feel forced, impersonal, and they go on for hours – at exactly the time I should be putting my kids to bed.

Sensing that there were others who felt the same, Josh and I took matters into our own hands by becoming part of the team that created Cedars' Rock for Research, a summertime concert and family day in our backyard, which boasts a more accessible price tag, a food court with offerings from dozens of the city's top restaurants, activities for the kids, and wine and spirits for the adults. Over the years, performers such as Macy Gray have been part of the draw for thousands of donors, and Rock for Research now represents one of Cedars most important fundraising events.

The 'Ultimate List of Charitable Giving Statistics' from NP Source charts annual fundraising event attendance by generation. Its recent results show little variation, with 55% of Millennials attending at least one fundraising event per year compared to 56% of GenXers and 58% of Boomers.

Everyone still likes a party, it seems, or at least a live event. And for organizations, especially those willing to embrace (as Cedars did) alternatives to the age-old gala, that means real opportunity.

Events Were Always Part of My Plan

Decades ago, I ran an art gallery in West Hollywood where I would sometimes host charitable events, sell the art on the walls, and then donate the profits to charity. That may have been something of an initiation for me, philanthropically speaking, into the world of events and the potential they hold. But I suspect it goes much deeper.

I grew up with parents who loved to throw parties. Very often, they'd let me tend bar. This was the era of themed parties and quite a lot of drinking and fun, and aside from making a perfect martini, my job as their kid was to be hilarious – mostly because I was twelve years old, and mixing cocktails. It was a pretty special experience.

Fast forward to 2011 and the house (and frequent event site) that Josh and I acquired in Beverly Hills. Not only does the place have a ton of Hollywood history, which is its own kind of special, it's also like nothing I ever saw myself living in. It took us about a year to find it because we knew we'd need a large, flat lot for the bigger events we dreamed of holding, as well as a really big room.

Throughout our search, I'd been imagining the colonial mansion from the 1991 remake of *Father of the Bride*. I wanted something just like it: a place full of love, joy, and family and not a whiff of what you'd call 'precious.' Well, we ended up purchasing a large, flat lot in Beverly Hills, but the house that sat on this lot was unabashedly glam. I'm talking about loads of marble and gold, and walls papered in actual silk – raw, non-washable silk that was covered in our kids' fingerprints within about a minute of our taking ownership.

So, we set to work renovating. You'd think the goals 'homey' and 'event site' might be at odds, but we managed to pull it off, and I'm proud to say today that the house is an amazing place of family, community, *and* philanthropy. It's seen almost 200 events since 2011, everything from intimate salons with thirty people present (I'll get into the salon model at the end of the chapter) to our annual Rock for Research Summer Concert series for Cedars, where some 1,500 guests gather in the garden.

I'd love to travel back in time and tell that kid tending bar at her parents' parties that, one day, she'd have parties of her own, all kinds of parties that bring people together, increase awareness for causes *while* raising money for charity, and even include guests who are rock stars (Elton John) or academics (university chancellors and deans and RAND policy researchers) or ambassadors and statesmen (the Mayor of Jerusalem and many consuls general) or veterans (in this case, women veterans running for Congress).

ELTON JOHN AND WHY THIS
NEVER GETS OLD

I actually 'met' Elton John about six months before he came to the house, and the minute we learned that he'd be a special guest at the American Fertility Association event we were hosting, well, Josh started teasing.

I met Elton at a party called 'The Night Before.' This is an event that happens annually in Los Angeles on the evening before the Academy Awards, and all of its proceeds go toward supporting seniors and seniors' services via the good work of the Motion Picture & Television Fund. I'd heard of the event when I was working at the studios – all the Oscar-nominated celebrities go, and the whole thing is super casual – but I could never afford a ticket myself.

Well, Josh happened to receive an invite that year, and Elton was there, and I got a little excited. I didn't do anything terrible, but, evidently, security was keeping an eye on me. And so, Josh's joke, when we were preparing for the American Fertility Association event, was that we should also prepare for Elton to realize who I was, alert security a second time, and cancel.

He didn't, of course. He was lovely.

Believe me, nothing comes close to what you can accomplish in person when you've got a group and a goal and the will to make change. There's so much potential magic in cause-based events, and yet your typical sector favorites – charity gala, anyone? – are frequently underwhelming.

I'll never forget the experience, for example, of hearing Dr. Denis Mukwege speak at an event in our home. A Congolese gynecologist and Pentecostal pastor, he campaigns globally against the use of rape as a weapon of war. He's become the world's leading specialist in the treatment of wartime sexual violence, and the work he does (much of which focuses on educating health practitioners) is astounding.

Knowing he'd been nominated for a Nobel Prize – which, when it happens, is often an open secret, even though the list of nominees is supposed to be sealed for fifty years – was also astounding.

Dr. Mukwege didn't win the prize the year he visited us, but he remained on the nominee list. Not long afterward, the Iraqi Yazidi human rights activist Nadia Murad *also* came to our home to tell her story. And, in 2018, Nadia and Denis received the Nobel Peace Prize *together* on the basis of (according to the Nobel Committee's statement on the Nobel Prize website) 'their efforts to end the use of sexual violence as a weapon of war and armed conflict.'

For everyone who shared the experience of meeting them, and everyone moved by their work, that's magic.

The Big-Ticket Gala

The other day, I received yet another invitation to an event that's a whole different animal to the events we hold, so far as fundraisers go: the charity gala. Before I opened the envelope (you'll note that it came via snail mail), I saw the return address and right alongside it, the name of the charity.

I love this charity.

Still, I was in a quandary. The envelope had a custom wax seal that showed a tiny silver imprint of the organization's logo. Beautiful, right? And costly ... just like I knew the gala would be, as this sort of fancy packaging almost always signals 'gala.' But without even breaking the seal on the envelope and removing the invite inside, I started hoping I was already booked.

Why?

I'm not exactly sure when the word 'gala' replaced the words 'charity fundraiser,' but I suspect someone thought that it was more genteel. Unfortunately, it took us farther from the truth of what these parties are about – and as with every other aspect of fundraising, not being straight about what we're doing is counter-productive. As I said in Chapter Three, you can't fake the hustle.

Increasingly, donors like myself *also* can't fake our preferences for cultivation, engagement, and fundraising events, and galas don't rank high. Knowing what they cost, many of us would much rather you plan events that have a larger return on investment. All the more when these galas aren't fun. This is a frequent complaint in my circles as well, to the extent, actually, that many donors I know would rather pay *not* to attend a charity gala.

To return to the issue of cost, one of the worst-kept secrets in the sector is that many galas don't make money. My fundraiser friend Margot puts it this way: 'These events are very expensive to run, with most getting 50 cents on the dollar. Some think they're great for cultivation in fundraising because they bring people out and show them a good time, but lots of others feel that they're a waste of money. Why not just have a house party with good wine and appetizers or a gathering for your younger donors at a rooftop bar?'

Why indeed.

CONSIDERING A BIG-TICKET EVENT?

Forbes 'Entrepreneurs' contributor Devin D. Thorpe wrote a great piece recently called 'How to Organize the Perfect Fundraising Gala.' As research, Thorpe started a conversation – much of which was quoted in the article – with several leaders in the sector: Carla Javits, CEO of REDF (Roberts Enterprise Development Fund); Fred Reggie, CEO of Fred Reggie Associates; Jordan Levy, chief external relations officer for Ubuntu Pathways; Brett Durbin, CEO of Trash Mountain Project, and Derek Rapp, CEO of JDRF (Juvenile Diabetes Research Foundation).

The first thing these leaders discussed was how to determine whether galas are 'right' for an organization in the first place. Each of them conceded that the model can work, but only if certain conditions are met. I'll paraphrase some of those conditions here:

- Organizations must have an established base of supporters who are likely to get behind the idea of a gala, and work to promote it
- Similarly, organizations *can* expect the model to be successful, but only if there is 'demand,' among supporters, for a gala-type of event
- Organizations must determine ahead of time that volunteers will come forward, to support staff in gala planning
- Organizations must take stock of the overhead involved, and ensure that existing resources (including staff resources) can accommodate the added work
- Organizations might even consider discounting the idea of a gala unless they have access to a project manager who is capable of planning and organizing an event of this scale
- Organizations should be able to count on a full eighteen months' worth of lead time for their first, large-scale gala; likewise, those organizations with less time available for planning might want to consider a different type of event

It's a good list, in my opinion, but I've got one thing to add, and that's that organizations must also be willing to factor staffing costs when they go through the process of forecasting revenue. When you're looking at the prices of venues and caterers and florists, it's easy to forget that your payroll is a line item too – especially if you've got staff members who will more or less be seconded away from their existing roles for the duration of gala planning.

Despite the cost, many organizations, especially the larger ones, have galas annually. Almost *every* organization has a gala at some point. Naturally, they're banking on the fact that people like me will purchase tickets or tables.

When I do buy tickets or a table, I often bring guests who I think will enjoy learning something about the cause. Which, of course, is the point. Only this has backfired more than once on account of the gala being ridiculously long, painfully boring, a seeming vehicle for guilt-tripping guests into making spontaneous gifts publicly, as well as a platform for inappropriate speeches. Sometimes the speeches are even alienating in that they're full of in-crowd references or worse, *no* references whatsoever to the organization we're there to support.

Even when the program is professional, there's always one insupportable moment for me, and that's when organizers take to the podium to 'celebrate' the dollars they've raised for the cause. The kicker here is that the majority of these announcements refer to the *gross* amount of dollars raised via the gala, as opposed to the net. Given that the net (what's left after you factor in costs) is going to make the philanthropic difference, why does this happen?

It happens because most organizations don't want to broadcast the fact that these galas are so costly to run. All the more, since the point is fundraising. With larger nonprofits, the costs may be manageable. There are definitely organizations out there that make very good money with their well-run galas. But the public profile enjoyed by these larger organizations makes sponsorships easier to get (sponsorships being the lifeblood of successful galas) and the organizations' internal resources (such as dedicated event, marketing, and communications staff) can typically shoulder the amount of work that's involved. Among small and mid-size nonprofits, however, the average gala cost (per dollars raised) is significantly higher than other fundraising events.

These days, I make a habit of querying the nonprofits I support, post-gala, to really get a sense of an event's success. I congratulate organizers on their 'take' (which is always presented to guests as substantial) and then I ask them if the amount raised is gross or net. The answers I get range from 'I don't know' or 'I don't have the final numbers in yet' to the sort of silence that suggests they don't want to tell me.

When I press for details, it almost always becomes clear, either during the conversation or later, that the net amount raised wasn't substantial at all. In fact, once nonprofits factor in their internal staffing costs as well opportunity costs – math that's too rarely done – the case for such a costly event is pretty weak. Remember, the goal of the charity gala is fundraising.

It breaks my heart to see people work so hard for such a paltry return on investment. As a donor and board member, I also have to wonder about the financial implications for both the charity and its beneficiaries. Finally, I wonder why we bother. Is the gala just a glorified attempt to please and pander to donors?

A REVENUE MODEL FOR GALAS

That same, very useful *Forbes* article advises that you only go forward with a fundraising gala if you're confident that it will generate about a 60% profit margin for your organization. This means, for example, that if the *gross* revenue you can expect to collect from all sources (including donations made at the event itself) equals $100K, your expenses must be kept under $40K.

Stuff costs more in New York and London than it does, say, in Waterville, Maine. But your gross revenue breakdown, per Fred Reggie Associates, should not vary too much:

- Sponsorships: 10%
- Ticket sales: 40%
- Drawing/raffle: 10%

- Silent auction: 20%
- Live auction: 20%

Models such as this are helpful in that they encourage us to adequately plan. The issue I have with this particular breakdown is not so much that its figures are off, it's more that they're so very predictable. As you can see, ticket sales, at 40%, are meant to completely cover gala costs – since costs, as you'll recall, should *also* sit at 40%. But this means that much of the evening will be devoted to raising that additional 60% from donors, and that's not a lot of fun for anyone.

In fact, many organizations ditch the raffle and auction elements because of the resources they require and the time they take out of the program. Given this, my suggestion is to consider another revenue model that looks to sponsorships for 60% of your total.

In either case, it's a lot of pressure, so do think hard about whether it's worth it.

What This Donor Didn't Know About Gala Honorees

When I first arrived in the world of the charity gala – in other words, when I could afford the tickets and attend as a guest, or even purchase a table or sponsorship – I truly believed that if you were an honoree at one of these events, you'd done something special. What I now know as a seasoned donor is that most people are honored for their ability to bring money.

Certainly, honoring the guy who'll bring in the big bucks makes a certain amount of sense. We're in the business, after all, of raising funds. But this practice is not without problems, one of which is the fact that these types of honorees often tend not to be all that connected with the organizations doing the honoring. Maybe the companies they work for have come forward with a gift to the organization of, for example, $50K. (I once served on a board that would select as 'honoree' anyone whose company contributed this amount, the idea being that the good exposure for the company was worth it.)

When the highlight of a charity event – the honoree – has no connection to the cause, it sort of strips the whole thing of meaning. It adds an additional, transactional element to the gala, which I believe guests can sense, and it can be hard on the 'honored' donors, especially if they're unaware of the quid pro quo; that is, the 'understanding' that they'll write a big check.

What is it like from their perspective? In short, you get a call during which you're told that you have been identified as someone important and/or charitable enough to be honored at a big event. You're flattered. When asked whether or not you'll accept this honor, you likely *do* accept. Why wouldn't you? Then about a week later, you discover that the assumption is that you will either contribute or secure a large amount of money for the organization that's doing the honoring.

If you're meant to secure the gift as opposed to furnish it from personal funds, it's often (as I've said) by way of getting the company you work for to contribute. Or, you'll give the organization that's honoring you your personal contact list and agree to help 'work' this list by encouraging your friends to buy ads, tickets, and (ideally) sponsorships.

Evidently, you do these things for the honor of being honored.

What's super awkward, however, is that rarely does the development person who makes the initial call say anything other than, 'Can we honor you?' All the additional stuff is implied in what I've come to describe as the 'nudge, nudge, wink, wink' vernacular of fundraising. And so when you, the donor, discover the truth about the 'honor,' it's sort of too late to back down. You feel manipulated, and you wonder why the organization doing the honoring wasn't upfront about its expectations in the first place.

STORYTELLING, SPEECHES, AND SWAG

Here's my donor friend Teri on the importance of storytelling: 'Every charity event needs to tell a story that adds a sort of "plot" to the proceedings, a story arc, and that speaks to the reason we've come. There's nothing worse than seeing an event that's humming along get interrupted suddenly by an out-of-the-blue ask for money, or a bit of business or "administrivia" that frankly just empties the room.'

And here's donor-volunteer Carlos on speeches: 'At one event I helped organize recently, there were several speeches, and at least two of them were inappropriate and "off." Development people need to be able to see all speeches beforehand to ensure that they're on target and that they somehow actually connect to the organization we're there to support. Also, why are there no length restrictions? Two minutes per speech is usually ideal.'

Finally, my donor friend Rose on swag: 'You get a bagful of swag at these events that you give away immediately. That's wasteful. If donors really feel that they *need* something to take away, then they're missing the point. I'd rather that the organizations I support spend their money on things that will matter. I don't need a bag of goodies. I don't even need a fancy dinner.'

Let's go back for a moment to you, nonprofits, and why these expectations exist. We've explored the risks galas pose in terms of return on investment. So, you do what's required to make them profitable – I get that. The problem is, not being clear and in mutual agreement about an honorees' 'obligations' to your organization at the outset only increases the odds that they won't fulfill them. Which happens, probably all too often.

Now add to the mix a wild card: the possibility that your honoree (believing they've been chosen for the 'leadership' they've shown, or their work on behalf of your charity) decides to take control, 'running the show' in a manner that isn't in line with your plans or worse, your professionalism.

This happens too.

Maybe you lose money, on these occasions, or maybe you lose face – neither is good. Nor is it good when an ostensibly successful event (one that features a great honoree who delivers a heartfelt speech about the work of the organization to a roomful of potential new donors) doesn't generate the sort of uptake in gifts that you were hoping it would. When *this* happens, it's often because the nonprofit hosting the event failed to make meaningful connections with guests during the scant few hours it had to engage them.

For these reasons and others, the model is fraught. This is why I'm recommending alternatives. It's also why, as a donor, I'm far more likely to respond positively to an organization that *truly* honors when it honors – whether it's me at that podium, or someone else.

YOUR TYPICAL GALA COMPONENTS

Most organizations that choose to have a gala will also choose someone to be honored. Sometimes two or three people are honored, and each of these people will be expected to 'market' the gala to their contacts as well as either donate to the organization from personal funds or secure a gift by way of their companies.

Whether or not they have a connection to the people being honored, companies are frequently asked to 'sponsor' galas and gala tables are 'sold' as well.

Some organizations will ensure that there is great, top-level entertainment at their galas, but this isn't necessarily the norm. What *is* the norm is a good-sized venue; food, beverage and everything they entail in the way of catering and bartending; a committee of involved volunteers; an in-house events team and/or an outside event planner; and a good deal of marketing and communications support.

Organizations might produce an 'ad book' (in either print or digital formats) and they might also hold a raffle or auction, whether 'live' or 'silent' or both.

And, because of the ticket price, everything's supposed to be done to a very high standard. This runs the gamut from the quality of the paper that your invitations are printed on (invitations that also require a digital equivalent) to the selection of appetizers that you serve before dinner.

So, while 'a little party never hurt anybody,' do think carefully, nonprofits, about *this* type of party and what it entails. There are lots of alternatives.

The Rules of this Book Apply Here Too

I can't tell you how many times we've 'given' our house to a charity to host an event, only to be solicited by that charity during the event itself. People come to the event, they're happy, they leave, we're tired – on one occasion, I was in the middle of clean-up – and that's when a fundraiser will approach us and ask, basically, 'Where's my check?'

First of all, who writes checks?

In all seriousness, though, this is a problem. In so many ways, it reinforces one of my primary, philanthropic pain points, and that's the lack of humanity I see when fundraisers muscle in for the 'ask.' As for these particular solicitations, I'm put off by the fact that our generosity (with the house and the catering, not to mention the energy and time) seems inadequate.

You already know that I'm disinclined to support charities that relentlessly ask me for more. And if the ask for money is shifty – slid neatly into the end of a lunch date or an event that we've had at our home – I'm doubly offended.

Josh and I do so many events in our home, wonderful events with extraordinary guests and very gracious fundraisers. But there *are* people out there who tend to forfeit that grace around money, and it's enough to make me want to remind you here to think hard about how (and when) your organization asks for funds at an event – even if the event's purpose is raising them.

So be upfront about the fundraising component to any event you're planning. Engage meaningfully when you *do* ask and understand that people have limits.

I get that these limits can be hard to identify, but your transparency will help to establish them. I once got a call, for example, from a congressman's campaign staffer. She was phoning to invite me to a 'Q&A,' as she called it, a small gathering of engaged people who would likely enjoy asking questions of someone in Congress. You could ask about Syria, the staffer said, you could ask about taxes – anything you happened to want to know. I liked the idea and said I would go.

Prior to the event, I received an email from the woman outlining the 'cost' of the evening for guests. I'd practically grilled her over the phone (so interested was I in the format) and not once had she mentioned a price tag. Why? Well, probably because she wanted me in the room. This is understandable, of course, but come on! If you're going to charge, charge. Just tell us, please, and then maybe, if the price of attendance is high, refrain from asking for even more money in the middle of the event or at the end of the evening.

FOUR EASY EVENT INNOVATIONS

- **Query your database.** Look at the demographics of your donors and prospects to gauge their relative levels of interest in galas, for example, versus other types of fundraising events. It's often possible to trace a donor's event preferences along generational lines, but there are outliers too – so consider querying your donors directly. When Cedars did this, its donors returned feedback that expressed a strong desire for events that were much more casual, and that's how Rock for Research was born.

- **Mandate an end-time for your events.** I developed even more admiration for LA's social-justice based Liberty Hill Foundation when I learned that it had imposed a hard-and-fast rule around gala end times – 9:30 p.m., actually, which I think is perfect. The trick, if you do this, is sticking to it.

- **Offer recipients of your invitation an easy way out.** The idea here is to make it straightforward and honorable for recipients to 'decline' an invitation by giving them the option to underwrite event tickets for staff, supporters, grantees, students or volunteers. Do note, though, that if donors agree to this option, it's important to refrain from saying (either in person or over email) that you 'missed them at the event' or 'hope to see them next year.' A simple 'thanks' is all that's necessary for this alternative means of support.

- **Drive home your organization's mission.** Whether explicitly stated or just inferred, your organization's mission should occupy a through-line in every event you hold. If you don't connect your event to your *raison d'être*, as a charity, you've missed an opportunity to engage your supporters. But do note also that it isn't always about money. It's perfectly appropriate, for example, to mention volunteer opportunities to donors once you've got them in the room for a fundraiser. And *I* always love post-event emails, especially those that include a reminder of the highlights of the evening (short video works wonders in this regard) as well as a simple 'thanks again for coming.'

I'd also be remiss if I didn't mention professionalism. Decency too. I've had development people whose charities are holding events at our home get super demanding in advance about the food we're providing. I wonder if it would surprise those people to learn that I fuss about things being nice – just as anyone would, when expecting guests – and that their demands are actually hurtful.

I've also experienced situations where there *wasn't* much food. I'll never forget, for example, arriving home one evening to find my staff up in arms. They felt they'd been treated disrespectfully by representatives of the charity holding an event that evening at the house. To make matters worse, this charity hadn't arranged for the food it had promised. They'd provided chips and crudités alongside a copious bar – but nothing substantial. Guests had been ordering out for pizza!

Do these stories make you want to give? Trust? Engage? Party?

I didn't think so. I'm hoping, however, that the rest of this chapter will change your mind.

One Organization's Alternative to the 'Rubber Chicken' Dinner

I think you'd be hard-pressed to find any substantial number of Millennials who actually want to 'own' (or in other words, 'help' in some way to organize) one of your standard, old-school charity events. These events typically rely heavily on volunteers (see page 268) and they privilege wining and dining. Besides being busy with their careers as well all the other fabulous things that their lives involve, most Millennials, as per the research we've discussed, want a more 'front-line' engagement than traditional galas allow.

I share their thinking, as you're aware. But since we're looking a new era in the face, so far as philanthropy goes, it's useful to look at how this generation is creating alternatives to the gala model.

Recently, I attended an event in Venice, California, organized by the Australia-based nonprofit 10x10 Philanthropy. This is a crowdfunding 'for purpose organization' that's focused on empowering younger generations to get involved with grass-roots charities. The cool thing about 10x10 is that it organizes events that are run entirely by volunteers. The event space is donated (a Venice warehouse, in this case), as is the food and drink (there was so much food!), and, basically, guests get to network, have cocktails, and watch three charities take to the 'stage' to pitch their respective causes.

Every event that 10x10 hosts is managed by a project committee whose volunteer members invite ten friends or more – and since the price of admission is $100, this creates a pool with an average of just over $20K that's distributed to the participating charities at the end of the night. And there lies the beauty: total audience involvement, complete donor agency (in that guests decide individually where to direct their 'Charity Dollars'), and nearly 100% donation to cause.

When I followed up with Laurence Marshbaum, who co-founded 10x10 in 2013, a couple of months had passed since the Venice event, and he was back in his native Australia. Laurence has a whole other career in finance, but this was the beginning of 2020 and the Australian bushfires were continuing to devastate wide swathes of New South Wales. Anyway, Laurence was in the throes of planning a 10x10 event called the 'Bushfire Edition,' whose three participating charities perfectly illustrate the organization's mandate.

'We wanted to design a model that's equitable,' Laurence told me. 'One that reflects a cross-section of issues that we know our audience will care about.' This typically ensures that each charity pitching at a given event will resonate with *someone* in attendance, thus becoming the eventual beneficiary of the person's 'Charity Dollars.' It also appeals 'to all the young people out there who are trying to be more thoughtful about the way they give their money.'

For example, 10x10's 'Bushfire Edition' featured Blaze Aid (an organization that sets up camps in fire-affected communities that equip teams of volunteers to rebuild fences, getting farming regions back on their feet); the Community Health Infrastructure and Resilience Fund of Mallacoota (which focuses on helping young people affected by the trauma of the bushfires in a town that was almost entirely wiped out at the end of 2019); and Science for Wildlife (whose aim is to increase drinking stations and food drops to koalas, kangaroos, and other fire-affected wildlife, and also re-introduce surviving animals to the wild).

Isn't that amazing? In this scenario, we may *think* we know what we'd do with our 'Charity Dollars' if we had tickets to 'Bushfire Edition,' but the Shark-Tank model lets us change our minds. I asked Laurence if he felt that there was anything to the criticism (see page 135) that such an obviously competitive framework pits charity against charity, and this was his response:

> First, money tends to be divided fairly equally among participating charities at these events. Also, we all still operate within a free-market system. Organizations that can best evidence their impact and professionalize the way they express themselves and their story – they do well. But if 10x10

can help upscale *all* participating charities in terms of these skills, that's a value-add. We want charities to go out there afterward and better connect with donors. We want them to be able to tell their stories more effectively and ultimately raise more money.

Laurence refers to 10x10 as an 'ecosystem,' one that already has a footprint globally. I'm not at all surprised.

There's a real shift that's happened among members of the current generation. They're thoughtful about how they give their time; they want to know a lot about where they give their money and they really want transparency. I'm not sure the old philanthropic model, the gala model that was about having a good time, resonates with this generation. Maybe even any generation.

So, to the extent that I can inspire them – inspire communities of volunteers all over the world to come forward and be a part of the 10x10 movement – that's time well spent.

On Remembering Our Reasons for Doing This

Laurence's comment about ecosystems reminded me of an experience I had with Josh several years ago, when he shared one of his fellowship readings for the Aspen Global Leadership Network. The reading described the early days of the abolitionist movement and it was pretty affecting – so much so that

I look to it for inspiration when I consider the potential in any event or gathering whose goal is social change.

For those who aren't familiar with this period in American history, I recommend you see the documentary *13th* (a name that's easy to remember when you realize it refers to 'Amendment XIII' to the US Constitution, which abolished slavery and involuntary servitude, except as punishment for a crime).

The background is that, in the years after the slaves were freed, the economy in this country was overwhelmed. You'd think that folks would do the right thing by properly rehiring the many people who had previously worked as slaves, but that's not what happened. The Southern States set about criminalizing minor offenses so that they could arrest the freed men, and when they couldn't pay the fines that were attached to their minor offenses, put them to work. These men were basically sent back to the slaveowners on a kind of furlough from prison.

One of the really messed-up things that came out of the situation was the equivalent of a modern-day ad campaign, which depicted African Americans as rapists and criminals. As one line of response to this infamy, people in the North started holding salons – here's where you'll see where I'm going with this – where whites and African Americans would gather together in someone's home or even a banquet hall and engage in dialogue. This dialogue was intended to right people's misconceptions on the one hand (for example, about what it meant to be black) and also work toward change.

What gets me about this salon model is that it takes a goal (let's say it's fighting injustice) and, instead of throwing money at this goal, it works *toward* it through gathering and learning. That's the potential of any charity event and it's what I wanted our home to be able to accommodate even before we purchased it. I had all sort of reasons for wanting this, most of which are central to what Timothy Seiler from the Lilly Family School of Philanthropy would call my 'philanthropic ambitions' (see page 88).

And while I may have realized these ambitions, at least in part, it saddens me to see what many events have become in the charitable sector. So very often, you go to a thing, you hear a pitch, and you give money. If you don't give money – well, at least your butt was in the seat of a not-empty room.

Is that really philanthropy?

What *I* propose instead is that we move the needle on our causes by privileging learning. If your organization is dealing with pending legislation that threatens a school, why not hold an event that encourages people to *learn* about why it's so threatening? If guests at the event are afterward inclined to give (and I suspect they'll be more inclined than they would be otherwise), great. If not, try again.

Or, consider partnering with other charities to stage a version of Laurence's approach with 10x10. As you've read, that model makes learning imperative. And sure, it involves a charge for admission. But guests only 'spend' their charitable dollars after a certain of amount of knowledge-sharing.

HOSTING YOUR OWN SALON

Philanthropy has always been an important element of salons via the idea of patronage, regardless of whether that patronage supported a writer (Honoré de Balzac), a musician (Frédéric Chopin) or a cause.

I'm always surprised, therefore, that salons aren't more popular with charities today. It's not difficult to host one once you realize that they're really the equivalent of a small-ish party or fundraiser whose primary focus is conversation. Any one of us could simply query a nonprofit we care about (or work for) about what sort of appetite they have for expanding their reach. Then, set a date, invite some friends, have your friends invite friends, and pull up some chairs in your living room.

Smaller nonprofits with less of a presence in their geographic areas may need to consider these events 'friend-raisers' instead of fundraisers, but that's okay, as we all need to educate others and build a base of supporters before we're able to raise money.

Salons should actually be an important part of any organization's awareness strategy, right alongside the online efforts to increase awareness that sector experts discuss at length. And take it from me, the chance to learn about a cause face-to-face from the leaders and/or beneficiaries who are best acquainted with it – that's golden. That's how you root an organization within the community it serves while also growing that community on behalf of your cause.

You'll probably laugh, but, in doing the research for this section, I came across a definition of my favorite model when it comes to charitable events, which you've probably already guessed is the salon. Anyway, this particular characterization of salons insisted that they always involve an 'inspiring host.' I'm not about to ask you to look to me for inspiration (Josh and I usually rely on our guests for that), but do give the model some thought. We're pretty loyal to it – for example, we very rarely charge for events at our home – because we've seen how effective it can be in increasing support for a cause.

Besides, salons have long been identified as an historical driver in the development of ideas – especially those relating to the public sphere – as well as the marshalling of action, where action is needed. Add dollars to this approach (again, there's $121 billion sitting in DAFs, at the time of this writing, that has yet to go out to charities) and you're looking at a paradigm shift in philanthropy.

I hope you'll join me in welcoming it.

NINE

GIVING THANKS AND 'SAVING GIVING'

Welcoming a New Era Together

When we moved to our new neighborhood and started our twins at the local public school, we got an email soliciting funds for the PTA. Naturally, I agreed to donate. I had no idea what was appropriate in terms of an amount, but, given what I was 'saving' relative to private-school tuition, I went for the highest option on offer – $10K. I suppose I thought that, for a school in Beverly Hills, a lot of parents would be doing the same.

What I didn't realize was that nobody gave to the PTA at that level. Josh and I were the only ones. I discovered this when the school circulated an email thanking its donors by name (hundreds of us were included) and also dividing our names into giving categories. Our names sat alone in the top category.

The thing is, we had no idea that the school would be recognizing our contribution at the dollar level, as opposed to just naming us among its many contributors. Nobody asked us if we wanted this kind of public recognition – it was just an assumption made by someone at the school. And as newcomers to both the school and the community, having our names at the top of this sort of mass communication made us deeply uncomfortable. Also, because the words 'Thanks to our wonderful donors!' (as well as those donors' names) had been added to the footer on all official school email, there was a period afterward during which we experienced this discomfort weekly. I appreciate that, at the end of the day, the gesture came from a good place. But it remains a great example of how important it is that organizations *ask* their donors how they'd like to be thanked.

My first big gift of $1M (see 'A Deal with God' on pages 13–16) elicited a similarly misguided response. Afterward, the temple that received the gift organized ten different events whose apparent purpose was, among other things, to thank me publicly. Everything was choreographed, down to the not-quite-accurate framing of these functions as 'volunteer appreciation,' and I eventually had to admit to the organizers that I had zero desire to be dragged on stage again for yet another display of public gratitude. Besides, I deeply resented having to cut short evening family time in order to attend these events.

Nonprofits, believe me when I tell you that the gratitude you express to your donors can absolutely bring them closer to you, your staff, and your cause. Or it can drive them away. (You already know, I'm sure, that if you don't thank *this* donor when she gives you something – whether it's a banana or a gift to your charity – she's going to be offended.) That said, I won't be filling these final pages with stats that show how the system sometimes fails to thank its donors effectively, or at all, as we looked at those stats in Chapter Seven.

Instead, I'll invite you to use this last chapter to consider what gratitude means, tactically and fundamentally, to a sector built on giving.

Gratitude: It's the Happy Ending We Deserve

I had the pleasure recently of meeting Larry C. Johnson, who parlayed a Yale University education in divinity and ethics into a storied career as a fundraising consultant. Several years ago, Larry's book, *The Eight Principles of Sustainable Fundraising*, was the subject of a *NonProfit Pro* article. One of my favorite lines from the article (a direct quote from Larry) is deceptively simple: 'You always offer to a donor more than you ask for.'

Gratitude is a gift. It's one of the 'offerings' that nonprofits are *able* to give donors, and that's why it's so terribly important. As Larry also says, 'Fundraising isn't really about money. Yes, money's involved. But it's really about relationships and fulfilled values and dreams.' If we embrace this idea – and it's definitely true for me – then it's sort of impossible to imagine a scenario in this sector where we either don't give thanks, or we use our thanks to manipulate donors into giving even more.

As everybody knows, this happens. Often, organizations will sneak an 'ask' into their annual messages of thanks in order to justify the costs of the mailing (or the resource drain of email) by framing the effort internally as 'revenue-generating.'

But donors aren't stupid, and if they perceive your thanks as insincere – if, for example, it comes with sad stories about additional need – well, that's sometimes worse than no thanks at all. Where it *is* appropriate to include an 'ask' with your thanks is in cases where donors have lapsed, and where a grateful reminder of these donors' past support can function as your 'opening' to invite them to renew.

FORTY-EIGHT HOURS TO BETTER RETENTION

What Your Donors Want ... and Why author Tom Ahern insists that charities can boost their first-time donor renewal rates by 400% – all they've got to do is issue a personal thanks to their first-time donors within 48 hours of receiving their gifts.

A whole lot of research supports this. Research also shows that, if, for example, you feel you lack the resources to send a really 'personal' thanks, you can always just pick up the phone (or use another, equally expedient mode of communication that you think suits your donor). Your percentage increase in first-year donor retention will likely still be significant, and your first-year retention revenue might increase as well.

Just consider this: DonorVoice's *The Agitator* gathered data from a 2017 'thank-you-call' program undertaken by

American public radio. In its inaugural year, the program (which involved saying a quick 'thanks' to donors via the telephone) generated a 56% increase in first-year donor retention and a 72% increase in first-year retention revenue.

As per Larry C. Johnson's advice, what you 'offer' to donors can be as straightforward as the respect you afford them when you *ask* them how they'd like to be thanked. In fact, offering your curiosity to donors – so long as you do it sincerely – is almost always a gracious act. With online donors, for example, with whom you (as fundraisers) typically don't get any face time, consider sending a follow-up query by email or phone. Here, you can ask donors (while you're thanking them) if they'd like more information about the organization or if there are programs that interest them specifically.

I actually save all the meaningful cards and letters that I've received over the years from charities. I should have more of these than I do, given the number of organizations we support, but my point here is that not only do these gestures matter, they also needn't be elaborate. One fundraiser I know sends handwritten postcards – sometimes on public holidays or giving anniversaries, and sometimes out of the blue – that basically just include a few words along the lines of, 'Your support made a difference this year.' I love that.

And for those of you worried about cost, email is a great alternative to snail mail in that it also allows for spontaneity.

I love being surprised by a charity that gets in touch with me with a short update or anecdote about, for example, a program I've funded, because these messages 'read' as an expression of gratitude. (By the same token, my friend Theresa, who is a longtime Big Brothers Big Sisters donor, is moved to tears every year by the photos she gets – sent with little fanfare, over email – that show her 'kids' enjoying their first swim at summer camp.)

THE THANKS I DIDN'T EXPECT

Back in summer 2018, I donated a bunch of frequent flier miles to the organization IfNotNow (see pages 118–19). I've mentioned non-cash donations at various points in these pages, but this particular donation was unique for all sorts of reasons, not the least of which was the thanks it yielded afterward – something I'll never forget.

The short story is that IfNotNow (an organization, as I explained earlier, that's trying to evolve our 'conversation' about Israel) decided to encourage several members of its movement to participate in a Birthright Israel trip. You may recall my discussing Birthright Israel in Chapter Six, in relation to Michael Steinhardt (see 'The New Norm?' on pages 193–5). Birthright Israel sponsors free summer trips to Israel for Jewish young adults – but the education it gives them, once there, is often one-sided and highly curated.

These young travelers, supporters of the principles of IfNotNow, basically undertook peaceful but 'disruptive' tactics on their Birthright Israel trips. They tried to engage genuinely with the program by asking questions about the Occupation, querying the program's itinerary, and also letting it be known that they were interested in a more fulsome version of the history of the region. Things came to a head on a bus tour, when several of them asked for a more accurate map than the one they'd been given, which neglected to include any reference to the existence of the West Bank.

Their tour guide responded by telling them explicitly that, on Birthright Israel trips, participants receive the version of the truth that the Israeli government and/or the organization's funders want to tell. And, if they didn't like this version, they should leave immediately, and find a narrative they *did* like. So that's what they did (after filming the interaction, which they'd later share on social media). As a result, their deposits were rescinded by Birthright, and their flights home (another 'free' component of every trip) were cancelled. For its part, Birthright maintained that it was an 'apolitical project' and interference with tours for political objectives could lead to the forfeit of deposits and plane tickets.

When I was approached by IfNotNow regarding the plight of these stranded travelers (who not only couldn't afford the price of airfare, but also had jobs to get back to, or school), I offered to give them my air miles. My contact at IfNotNow had let me know that these young adults went to

Israel with the goal of demanding a more complete picture of Israel from Birthright – and I couldn't *not* support that.

What I didn't expect were the logistics involved in arranging flights using frequent-flier miles for five stranded people, none of whom I'd met. I was on the phone and on email for nearly 24 hours, but we got it done. And it wasn't until I received thanks from the travelers by way of a simple video in which each of them spoke of the significance of the trip – what it had meant to be there, and what my support had meant – that I understood it too. It was really meaning-ful, Video provided an unusual, vivid, and very personal way for me to *see* my gift recipients (and hear them speak) as well as feel the impact of what I'd given them.

I highly recommend this form of thanks and hope to see it used more often in the future.

In our sector especially, gratitude often involves an exchange. It's a cycle of asking and giving and thanking that brings us back yet again to relationships. But fundraising is a process and, as our relationships change within this process, so too will the way we give thanks. The Lilly Family School of Philanthropy's Timothy Seiler puts it this way:

The beginning of the process is somewhat impersonal. We attract a first-time donor through a means such as email, direct mail, telephone call or special event. At this level, we're just getting to know them. But once someone has made a gift and thus indicated their interest in the cause, our responsibility as fundraisers is to acknowledge that interest appropriately. We hold ourselves accountable by reporting back to the donor on the use and impact of the gift, and then we invite the donor to give again.

As the donor gives more (and often larger) gifts, the relationship moves in the direction of the personal. This is where letters are sent or personal notes are exchanged, and where donor visits happen as well. We come to know the individual, not the name on the piece of paper or the guest list for an event, and the relationship grows. It's a process that unfolds over time.

SO MANY WAYS TO EXPRESS YOUR GRATITUDE TO DONORS

Make a call to say thanks

Write a handwritten note card

Show curiosity

Send a personal email

Be transparent

Send a welcome package

Acknowledge an anniversary

Remember a birthday

Send a text if you're rushed

Thank when it's not expected

Organize a site tour

Be thoughtful

Send a progress report

Show impact creatively

Make a video

Change who's doing the thanking

Send photos

Acknowledge a personal

success

Be spontaneous

Share your knowledge

Do a social media shout

out

Connect them with others

Organize a gratitude

campaign

Send a letter

Celebrate a gift to another

charity

Surprise by not asking for

money

Naming as Thanks ... or Currency?

Nonprofits frequently use naming opportunities to 'sweeten the pot' with prospective donors, and who can blame them? Many of these organizations are competing with one another for crucial support from a limited pool, and putting a donor's name on the wall of a big museum, for example, is a pretty enduring form of gratitude. The irony is that named buildings (especially those connected with prestigious institutions) can also create competition among donors. This takes 'keeping up with the Joneses' to a whole new level, but if it helps to keep the lights on at a hospital or funds a school of the arts, I'm all for it.

I happen to think that vanity doesn't motivate the majority of major donors. Yes, ego is a driver for some (as, sadly, is the desire for good 'PR' in advance of a court case – see page 61), but the prospect of a named building is much more frequently attached in a donor's mind to legacy. We'll get to that shortly.

In the meantime, here is my fundraiser friend Sheila with a rather compassionate take (and a frustrated one, too) on the ego-driven donor:

> There is one donor I know who is relatively young. She isn't married and she doesn't have kids and she wants so very badly to be seen. She owns multiple homes, and hosts big parties, which always go on for days and are meant to be enormously fun for all involved. Anywhere this donor goes, she wants to see her name on things. Everything about her persona screams, "Look at me!" And so, with her philanthropy, she wants the biggest bang for her buck. She wants to know what the minimum gift is for the maximum publicity, it's that simple an equation.

Once you start looking for this sort of thing, you see it everywhere – from the names on our biggest buildings to the dedication on a bench at the park. I saw an episode in the Showtime series *Billions* the other day that depicted fictional Bobby Axelrod (hedge-fund magnate and billionaire) in a bit of meltdown over the name of the equally fictional 'Ellis Eads Hall.' Bobby ('The Bob' or 'The Rod' or 'The Axe') just can't cope with the fact that somebody with as ridiculous a name as 'Ellis Eads' got to be associated 'with such a great building.'

But it's what Bobby does next (and the megabucks he offers, to get the name on the building's monument replaced with *his* name) that speaks to the idea of legacy. Specifically, buying a legacy. There's nothing wrong with this in theory, and I'd hazard to guess that most of us can relate to the desire to leave something of ourselves behind – whether it's our kids, our work or our charity. Still, philanthropists *and* philanthropies need to think hard (see page 300) about the ethics of naming, especially in this public sphere.

Also, recognition isn't always a driver. When my brother gave to his synagogue, for example, he wasn't comfortable with the idea of his name being used. 'This is what's done,' he was told. So, he wrote a poem – and that's what appears on the building. I think he knows (and *I* know) that our father would be proud. It's the same with Greer Social Hall, which was the result of my own donation to Temple Emanuel in Beverly Hills. I had mixed feelings about the name (because I don't particularly relish being *that* rich family), but I also didn't want to be a jerk. And it's okay, I've decided. As a family, it's part of our story.

ACKNOWLEDGMENT GIFTS MADE IN MEMORY OR TRIBUTE

I have a good friend whose colleague died suddenly last year. This friend works at a nonprofit, as did her colleague, but the nonprofit's memorial program for donations made in honor or memory of someone was really complicated. People at the organization *wanted* to give in her memory, but they were also grieving – it was just too much to navigate.

'10 Best Tribute and Memorial Fundraising Tips for Nonprofits,' published by *Donorbox* recently, contains some useful advice about this very sensitive area of fundraising. I wasn't surprised to learn, for example, that 33% of donors worldwide give tribute gifts, with the top occasions being memorials (43%) and birthdays (25%). Tribute gifts are also often considered a bit of a 'gateway' to legacy giving (or testamentary gifts).

So it's in your interest, nonprofits, to consider starting or refining your own tribute/memorial program, and all the more if your organization naturally 'works' with this type of giving (an animal shelter, for example, can invite donors to give in memory of pets they have lost).

Here, paraphrased, are some of my favorite pieces of advice from *Donorbox*:

- Be sure to highlight how tribute donations help you pursue your mission so that this sort of giving feels 'right' to donors who may be struggling with the loss of a loved one.
- Invite donors to notify the recipient of the donation themselves. For memorial gifts, donors may want to send a note to the decedent's family or even post a comment online.
- Consider peer-to-peer fundraising. Here, you can enable donors to set up a tribute page or an 'in memory of' page to collect donations from family and friends.
- Keep things simple. Give donors the ability to indicate (for example, via online form) whether their gifts are 'in

honor of' or 'in memory of.' Invite them to name the person being honored, as well as to decide whether they'd like family friends of the honoree to be alerted about the tribute.

- Give donors the option to make regular or recurring gifts in the name of a loved one.

- Consider branding the program. This stuff can be very sensitive, and creating a distinct look and feel for your tribute and memorial giving program – so long as it's still linked to the 'mother' brand – will really help set the right tone.

- Accept that it can be emotionally challenging for fundraisers to facilitate these types of gifts and do what you can to smooth the process. For example, an acknowledgment letter template for memorial gifts can be created in advance and personalized on a case-by-case basis.

PETER KAROFF ON THE 'ART OF LOVE' IN PHILANTHROPY

For those who don't know him, the late Peter Karoff earned his nickname as 'Father of Philanthropic Advising' by way of his work at The Philanthropic Initiative and Tufts University, as well as his book *The World We Want: New Dimensions in Philanthropy and Social Change*. Writing in the *Stanford*

Social Innovation Review before he passed, Karoff describes what happens when real empathy is established in gift relationships – empathy that moves these relationships out of the arena of power and dependency and into something much deeper.

When this happens, the gift moves beyond the hard evidence that defines it (money and terms and measurable impact) or the transaction that enabled it. Karoff writes: 'Its mystery is in the relationships between donor, recipient, and the community of interest that is served. It is a dynamic that operates on multiple levels. One level is contractual and may be spelled out in considerable detail – for example, a multi-year grant to a youth organization based on research, data, and measurable evidence. Call this level science. But it is the relationships between the parties who have an interest that makes or breaks the success of a program. These relationships flow between the organization's staff, the youth involved in the program, parents and extended families, and powerful peer-groups, all of which intersect within a community culture. These are the "influences" of a pretty complex system that is part cognitive, part non-cognitive; and therein lies the "love" factor. Therein lies the art.'

It's hard to talk about love when we're also talking about money (see page 85) and that's why Karoff's words are so affecting. *I* love the idea that there's a 'mystery' in gift relationships, and that if you add enough empathy, the outcome moves beyond measurable evidence.

'Saving Giving' is on Us

The cold call, the compliments, the two-hour lunch – I'm quite sure it all started because someone understood intuitively that the practice of philanthropy involves relationships. But the old ways are no longer working, and most donors don't want to complain. As per a recent article in *Forbes*, the richest 10% now hold 70% of total household wealth, up 60% from 1989. Most donors probably figure that nobody wants to hear a rich person kvetch about how hard it is to give money away.

I'm sure they're right.

Yet, as you well know, in the decade since becoming a major donor, I've been lied to, manipulated, and strong-armed – all in the name of giving. With this kind of maneuvering and these sorts of tactics, I worry that donors will walk (they're already doing so) and the nonprofits we love will crumble.

There's a lot of talk these days about the idea of 'disruption' overstaying its welcome. Call it what you will – we can even just call it 'big change' – but applied to philanthropy, it's worth undertaking. *Forbes* calls disruption 'the most influential business idea' of the last century, and quotes disruption guru Clayton Christensen (who happened to pass away as I was writing this chapter) when distinguishing 'disruption' from 'innovation.' Christensen says that 'a disruption displaces an existing market, industry or technology and produces something new and more efficient and worthwhile. It is at once destructive and creative.'

I'm willing to bet that any big change in the way philanthropy is practiced – the 'destructive' piece in the Christensen quote – is going to make a whole lot of people extremely uncomfortable. But as Alan Solomont, Dean of the Jonathan M. Tisch College of Civic Life at Tufts University, told me: 'The institutions that depend on us are going to have to find new ways of attracting support. And they will, largely. And those that don't will die.'

Besides, any change that replaces the 'old' with the 'new' is by nature creative (as well as disruptive, at least if you're defining the word broadly). In our sector, I see this change at work among members of the younger generations who are already finding their own creative spaces in which to engage their philanthropy. Not only are they forming alternative communities of giving, but the way they're *thinking* about giving – and executing on this thinking – is entirely new. As Alan also says, 'Right now, so many young people are coming back into the civic space and into politics. They'll figure out a way to get into philanthropy as part of that.'

My adult children are already living what Alan describes, and it's amazing to watch. One of my biggest fears when we made our fortune was that having money would change the kids – especially the twins, who have never really known life without it. Empathy is essential to any ethos of giving and caring, and I wanted *all* our kids to have it and also use it in the service of others. When, years before, my middle daughter was diagnosed with cancer, I learned that any kid can experience an empathy boost simply by sitting in the ER of a children's hospital. So I knew there were ways that we could *teach* our kids compassion, just as I knew that this education would focus on giving.

Since then, it's been interesting to watch them mature in their philanthropy, share stories, and tips, and even delight in the discovery of meaningful causes. Our youngest son, for example, has had a Donor Advised Fund since he was five years old. At first, he only wanted to give if he could get something back, and he loved the World Wildlife Federation for its incentive promise to send a different stuffed animal for every donation he made. Josh and I used to marvel at the collection he amassed – an Arctic hare, an Atlantic puffin, a loggerhead turtle, a fennec fox – and although his giving has evolved in the years since, I like to think of that collection of animals as the beginnings of a community he was forming with his own philanthropy.

In a sector whose primary concern is the welfare of others, community is essential. And as donors and fundraisers, the more we experience our *own* community as enriching and authentic – by way of our work, our money, our service, and our impact – the more effective we'll be.

Everybody wins in this scenario, and so does philanthropy.

All that's left for us to do is make it happen.

SOURCES AND FURTHER READING

Prologue

The Chronicle of Philanthropy (March 17, 2020). 'What We Have
Learned From Crises and Can Use in Coronavirus Age':
https://www.philanthropy.com/article/
What-We-Have-Learned-From/248260

Giving USA 2019 (published June 18, 2019): https://givingusa.
org/tag/giving-usa-2019/

One

National Center for Charitable Statitistics (NCCS): 'The
Nonprofit Sector in Brief 2018': https://nccs.urban.org/
publication/nonprofit-sector-brief-2018

Sources relating to cuts to funding:

For arts cuts, from the *Washington Post* (March 18, 2019): https://www.washingtonpost.com/lifestyle/style/for-third-year-in-a-row-trumps-budget-plan-eliminates-arts-public-tv-and-library-funding/2019/03/18/e946db9a-49a2-11e9-9663-00ac73f49662_story.html

For social services cuts, from the Center on Budget and Policty Priorities (February 14, 2018): https://www.cbpp.org/research/federal-budget/trump-budget-deeply-cuts-health-housing-other-assistance-for-low-and

For scientific research, from *Science* (February 13, 2020): https://www.sciencemag.org/news/2020/02/how-congress-could-reverse-cuts-trump-s-budget-request-nsf

Lilly Family School of Philanthropy Philanthropy Panel Study (PPS) data, as presented on the platform Generosity for Life: http://generosityforlife.org/

Business Insider, 'Millennials are set to inherit record wealth – and the way they manage it will be unprecedented' (August, 2017): https://www.businessinsider.com/millennials-inherit-record-wealth-manage-money-technology-2017-8

Giving USA 2019 (published June 18, 2019): https://givingusa.org/tag/giving-usa-2019/

Pew Research Center 2014 Religious Landscape Study: https://www.pewforum.org/2015/05/12/americas-changing-religious-landscape/

The New York Times (November 3, 2016), 'Donations to Religious Institutions Fall as Values Change': https://www.nytimes.

com/2016/11/06/giving/donations-to-religious-institutions-fall-as-values-change.html

The 2018 U.S. Trust Study of High Net-Worth Philanthropy (conducted in partnership with The Indiana University Lilly Family School of Philanthropy): https://www.privatebank.bankofamerica.com/articles/2018-us-trust-study-of-high-net-worth-philanthropy.html

Inside Philanthropy (November 29, 2017), 'Are We Living in a Golden Age of Charitable Giving? Hardly': (https://www.insidephilanthropy.com/home/2017/11/29/falling-charitable-giving-trends)

Callahan, David, *The Givers: Wealth, Power, and Philanthropy in a New Gilded Age* (Knopf, 2017)

Barclays Private Bank, 'Barriers to Giving: Research into the evolving world of philanthropy': https://privatebank.barclays.com/content/dam/privatebank-barclays-com/en-gb/private-bank/documents/what-we-offer/philanthropy/barriers-to-giving-ibim9550.pdf

'Chinese and Chinese American Philanthropy', 2017, research conducted by the UCLA Luskin School of Public Affairs, the Long U.S.–China Institute at UC Irvine, and the nonprofit Asian Americans Advancing Justice-Los Angeles: https://www.globalchinesephilanthropy.org/gcpi/report

The Chronicle of Philanthropy (August 13, 2018), 'Donors of Color Are Not "New" or "Emerging." We've Been Giving All Along.': https://www.philanthropy.com/article/Opinion-Donors-of-Color-Are/244252

The Chronicle of Philanthropy (April 2, 2012), 'The Cost of High Turnover in Fundraising Jobs': https://www.philanthropy.com/article/The-Cost-of-High-Turnover-in/226573

The Chronicle of Philanthropy (August 4, 2019), 'Why Fundraisers Leave, and How to Keep Them': https://www.philanthropy.com/interactives/20190802_Fundraisers

NonProfit Pro (August 29, 2019), 'The Rise of Women in Philanthropy': https://www.nonprofitpro.com/article/the-rise-of-women-in-philanthropy/

Better Business Bureau (October 25, 2018), 'Do People Trust Charities? Study by BBB's Give.org Uncovers Pitfalls': https://www.bbb.org/article/news-releases/18754-do-people-trust-charities-study-by-bbbs-giveorg-uncovers-pitfalls

Bloomberg (November 12, 2019), 'Wealthy Amass Record $121 Billion in Tax-Sheltered Accounts': https://www.bloomberg.com/news/articles/2019-11-12/wealthy-amass-record-121-billion-in-tax-sheltered-accounts

MarketWatch (June 18, 2018), 'American donations to charity show widening gap between rich and poor' (NB: article sources 'Revenue Service Business Master Files, Exempt Organizations (2006–16))': https://www.marketwatch.com/story/americans-give-more-to-charitybut-recent-donations-show-widening-gap-between-rich-and-poor-2018-06-16

Business Insider (August 2017), 'Millennials are set to inherit record wealth – and the way they manage it will be unprecedented': https://www.businessinsider.com/millennials-inherit-record-wealth-manage-money-technology-2017-8

Bloomerang, 'Major Gift Fundraising By The Numbers': https://bloomerang.co/blog/infographic-major-gift-fundraising-by-the-numbers/

Goldseker, Sharna, and Moody, Michael, *Generation Impact: How Next Gen Donors Are Revolutionizing Giving* (Wiley, 2017), p. 2.

Two

Independent (January 5, 2011), 'Love of 'Brigadoon' inspires Vegas tycoon to leave fortune to Scotland': https://www.independent.co.uk/news/people/news/love-of-brigadoon-inspires-vegas-tycoon-to-leave-fortune-to-scotland-2176161.html

Forbes (March 5, 2019), 'Billionaires: The Richest People in the World': https://www.forbes.com/billionaires/#52860a38251c

Spectrem Group: Voice of the Investor, 'New Spectrem Group Study Reveals the Wealthiest U.S. Investors Are Becoming Younger and Their Numbers are Growing – January 22, 2019': https://spectrem.com/Content/press-release-new-spectrem-study-reveals-the-wealthiest-us-investors-are-becoming-younger-012219.aspx

Credit Suisse, Global Wealth Report 2019: https://www.credit-suisse.com/about-us-news/en/articles/media-releases/global-wealth-report-2019--global-wealth-rises-by-2-6--driven-by-201910.html

Edelman Trust Barometer Global Report, 2019: https://www.edelman.com/sites/g/files/aatuss191/files/2019-02/2019_Edelman_Trust_Barometer_Global_Report.pdf

NonProfit Quarterly (June 18, 2019), 'Giving USA 2019: Most
 Nonprofits Will Need to Work Harder for Their Money':
 https://nonprofitquarterly.org/giving-usa-2019-most-
 nonprofits-will-need-to-work-harder-for-their-money/

Bloomberg (November 12, 2019), 'Wealthy Amass Record $121-
 Billion in Tax-Sheltered Accounts': https://www.bloomberg.
 com/news/articles/2019-11-12/wealthy-amass-record-121-
 billion-in-tax-sheltered-accounts

Giving USA 2019: https://givingusa.org/?utm_source=Google&
 utm_medium=D%2BC%20Ads&utm_campaign=Grant

The NonProfit Times (July 25, 2019), 'Schwabb Reports Grants Up
 By A Third': https://www.thenonprofittimes.com/grant/
 schwab-reports-grants-up-by-a-third/

Institute for Policy Studies (July 25, 2018), 'Report: Warehousing
 Wealth': https://ips-dc.org/report-warehousing-wealth/

The Millennial Impact Report: 10 Years, Looking Back: http://
 www.themillennialimpact.com/

Korn Ferry, 'The Charitable Giving Revolution': https://www.
 kornferry.com/insights/articles/philanthropy-revolution

CNBC Financial Advisor 100 (October 21, 2019), 'What the $68
 trillion Great Wealth Transfer means for advisors': https://
 www.cnbc.com/2019/10/21/what-the-68-trillion-great-
 wealth-transfer-means-for-advisors.html

Barron's June 26, 2019 analysis of the Wealth-X report,
 'Generational Shift: Family Wealth Transfer Report 2019: The
 Wealthy Will Transfer 12.4 Trillion by 2030': https://www.
 barrons.com/articles/the-wealthy-will-transfer-15-4-trillion-
 by-2030-01561574217

YCore website: www.ycore.org

Blackbaud Institute (April 24, 2018), 'The Next Generation of American Giving': https://institute.blackbaud.com/asset/the-next-generation-of-american-giving-2018/

Lilly Family School of Philanthropy (March 13, 2018), 'Adult Children – Especially Daughters – More Likely To Give To Charity If Parents Give': https://www.philanthropy.iupui.edu/news-events/news-item/adult-children%E2%80%94especially-daughters%E2%80%94more-likely-to-give-to-charitable-causes-if-parents-give.html?id=257

Giving USA 2019: https://givingusa.org/?utm_source=Google&utm_medium=D%2BC%20Ads&utm_campaign=Grant

Three

Grain (August 29, 2018), 'Toxic philanthropy: Wealthy US donors are influencing policy to serve their own interests': https://www.grain.org/en/article/6031-toxic-philanthropy-wealthy-us-donors-are-influencing-policy-to-serve-their-own-interests

Bank of America's 'Friends Again' report, as discussed in Forbes (October 17, 2017), 'Lending Someone Even Small Amounts of Cash Can Ruin a Friendship, Survey Finds': https://www.forbes.com/sites/sleasca/2017/10/17/pay-back-friends-app/#6eed1c247cf1

The New York Times (May 7, 2006), 'Money Changes Everything': https://www.nytimes.com/2006/05/07/fashion/sundaystyles/07friendss.html

Ramsay Solutions, 'Money, Marriage and Communication: The Link Between Relationship Problems and Finances': https://cdn.ramseysolutions.net/media/b2c/personalities/rachel/PR/MoneyMarriageAndCommunication.pdf?_ga=2.77674900.143793686.1583002164-546354625.1571091414

TED Talk, 'The way we think about charity is dead wrong': https://www.ted.com/talks/dan_pallotta_the_way_we_think_about_charity_is_dead_wrong

The New York Times (November 7, 2013), 'Gadfly Urges a Corporate Model for Charity': https://www.nytimes.com/2013/11/08/giving/gadfly-urges-a-corporate-model-for-charity.html

Pallotta, Dan, *Uncharitable: How Restraints on Nonprofits Undermine Their Potential* (Tufts University Press, 2008), p. xii

Klontz Consulting Group: Your Mental Wealth: https://www.yourmentalwealth.com/assessment/

The Chronicle of Philanthropy (October 15, 2019), 'Nonprofit Communications Don't Resonate With Donors': https://www.philanthropy.com/article/Nonprofit-Communications/247340

Four

Lisa's IfNotNow coverage:

The Jewish News of Northern California (March 29, 2017): 'How and why politics gets in the way of Jewish giving': https://www.jweekly.com/2017/03/29/how-and-why-politics-gets-in-the-way-of-jewish-giving/

Haaretz (December 4, 2016): 'L.A. Jewish Fund Refuses to
    Channel Donations to Anti-occupation Group': https://www.
    haaretz.com/us-news/l-a-jewish-fund-refuses-to-channel-
    donations-to-anti-occupation-group-1.5469671
Jewish Journal (December 1, 2016): 'Foundation fund nixes
    progressive donation': https://jewishjournal.com/news/
    los_angeles/212976/
The *Forward*: 'When Israel Politics Gets In The Way Of Jewish
    Charitable Giving': https://forward.com/news/367314/
    when-israel-politics-gets-in-the-way-of-jewish-charitable-giving/
The Chronicle of Philanthropy (October 17, 2018): 'How to Make
    the Case for General Operating Support': https://www.
    philanthropy.com/article/How-to-Make-the-Case-for/244808

Five

Fidelity Charitable, 'Time and Money: The Role of Volunteering in
    Philanthropy': https://www.fidelitycharitable.org/insights/
    volunteering-and-philanthropy.html

Six

Charity Navigator: www.charitynavigator.org
GuideStar by Candid: www.guidestar.org
Forbes (May 13, 2013), 'Locks of Love: $6 Million of Hair
    Donations Unaccounted For Each Year': https://www.forbes.

com/sites/quora/2013/05/13/locks-of-love-6-million-of-hair-donations-unaccounted-for-each-year/#16d384cb5fd0

CBSN San Francisco KPIX 5 (May 15, 2013), 'Bay Area Group Questions Donations to Locks of Love': https://sanfrancisco. cbslocal.com/2013/05/15/bay-area-group-questions-donations-to-locks-of-love/

The New Yorker (March 21, 2019), 'The Reckoning of Morris Dees and the Southern Poverty Law Center': https://www. newyorker.com/news/news-desk/the-reckoning-of-morris-dees-and-the-southern-poverty-law-center

The Chartered Governance Institute (ICSA): https://www.icsa. org.uk/

The New York Times (March 21, 2019), 'Michael Steinhardt, a Leader in Jewish Philanthropy, Is Accused of a Pattern of Sexual Harassment': https://www.nytimes.com/2019/03/21/ nyregion/michael-steinhardt-sexual-harassment.html

NYU Local (September 12, 2019), 'NYU Will Not Rename Steinhardt After Namesake Admitted to Making Inappropriate Remarks': https://nyulocal.com/ nyu-will-not-rename-steinhardt-after-namesake-admitted-to-making-inappropriate-remarks-8e044de6ba19

NYU Local (Mar 21, 2019), 'Michael Steinhardt Accused of Sexual Harassment by 7 Women': https://nyulocal.com/ michael-steinhardt-accused-of-sexual-harassment-by-7-women-800a0fc7dacf

Leading with Intent: 2017 BoardSource Index of Nonprofit Board Practices: https://leadingwithintent.org/

Harvard Business Review (June 4, 2019), 'Why You Should Create a "Shadow Board" of Younger Employees': https://hbr.org/2019/06/why-you-should-create-a-shadow-board-of-younger-employees

The New York Times (October 2, 2019), 'New Scrutiny of Museum Boards Takes Aim at World of Wealth and Status': https://www.nytimes.com/2019/10/02/arts/design/whitney-art-museums-trustees.html

Resource Generation: www.resourcegeneration.org

Solidaire: https://solidairenetwork.org/

The Chronicle of Philanthropy (September 3, 2019), 'Cleveland Clinic and Case Western University Raise More Than $275 Million in Joint Campaign': https://www.philanthropy.com/article/Cleveland-ClinicCase/247061

Seven

Bloomerang (January 8, 2020), A Guide to Donor Retention: https://bloomerang.co/retention

2018 Association for Fundraising Professionals (AFP) Fundraising Effectiveness Survey Report: http://afpfep.org/wp-content/uploads/2018/04/2018-Fundraising-Effectiveness-Survey-Report.pdf

2019 Association for Fundraising Professionals (AFP) Fundraising Effectiveness Survey Report: http://afpfep.org/reports/

Bank of America, 'The 2018 U.S. Trust Study of High Net-Worth Philanthropy conducted in partnership with the Indiana

University Lilly Family School of Philanthropy': https://www.privatebank.bankofamerica.com/articles/2018-us-trust-study-of-high-net-worth-philanthropy.html

Barclays Private Bank, 'Barriers to Giving: Research into the evolving world of philanthropy': https://privatebank.barclays.com/content/dam/privatebank-barclays-com/en-gb/private-bank/documents/what-we-offer/philanthropy/barriers-to-giving-ibim9550.pdf

The Chronicle of Philanthropy (November 5, 2019), 'Worried About More Than a Possible Recession': https://www.philanthropy.com/article/Habitat-for-HumanityIRC-/247423

plainlanguage.gov: an official website of the United States government: https://www.plainlanguage.gov/

The Chronicle of Philanthropy (May 15, 2018), '4 Steps to Strategic Communications': https://www.philanthropy.com/resources/checklist/4-steps-to-strategic-communica/6598/

Classy (May 20, 2019), 'Why Your Nonprofit Needs a Brand Book': https://www.classy.org/blog/nonprofit-brand-book/

Combined sources for text box on p. 251:

Classy, 'The State of Modern Philanthropy: Examining Online Giving Trends': https://www.classy.org/blog/the-state-modern-philanthropy-report/

NP Source, 'The Ultimate List Of Charitable Giving Statistics for 2018': https://nonprofitssource.com/online-giving-statistics/

Donorbox (April 9, 2018), 'Quick Tips to Create a Great Monthly Giving Program': https://donorbox.org/nonprofit-blog/great-monthly-giving-program/

Eight

NP Source, 'The Ultimate List Of Charitable Giving Statistics for 2018': https://nonprofitssource.com/online-giving-statistics/

Forbes (August 29, 2018), 'How To Organize The Perfect Fundraising Gala': https://www.forbes.com/sites/devinthorpe/2018/08/29/how-to-organize-the-perfect-fundraising-gala/#178e506579df

Nine

Johnson, Larry C., CFRE, *The Eight Principles of Sustainable Fundraising: Transforming Fundraising Anxiety into the Opportunity of a Lifetime* (Aloha Publishing, 2011)

NonProfit PRO (April 4, 2012), 'Larry C. Johnson: The 8 Principles of Sustainable Fundraising': https://www.nonprofitpro.com/article/larry-c-johnson-the-8-principles-sustainable-fundraising/all/

Ahern, Tom, *What Your Donors Want ... and Why* (Emerson & Church Publishers, 2017)

GuideStar Blog (January 29, 2018), 'How Quickly Should You Thank a New Donor': https://trust.guidestar.org/how-quickly-should-you-thank-a-new-donor

Donorbox Nonprofit Blog (May 20, 2019), '10 Best Tribute and Memorial Fundraising Tips for Nonprofits': https://donorbox.

org/nonprofit-blog/tribute-and-memorial-fundraising-tips-for-nonprofits/

Forbes (May 29, 2019), 'America's Humongous Wealth Gap is Widening Further': https://www.forbes.com/sites/pedrodacosta/2019/05/29/americas-humungous-wealth-gap-is-widening-further/#73eaae3542ee

Karoff, Peter (with Jane Maddox), *The World We Want: New Dimensions in Philanthropy and Social Change* (AltaMira Press, 2006)

Stanford Social Innovation Review (December 17, 2012), 'The Art of Love in Philanthropy': https://ssir.org/articles/entry/the_art_of_love_in_philanthropy#

Forbes (March 17, 2013), 'Disruption Vs. Innovation: What's The Difference?': https://www.forbes.com/sites/carolinehoward/2013/03/27/you-say-innovator-i-say-disruptor-whats-the-difference/#bbffc876f432

ACKNOWLEDGMENTS

This book, like many others, has had a long history. It started with an almost daily rant to my friends about my frustrations with the state of philanthropy. After several years of that, I decided my friends had suffered enough and started writing a book. I began to pitch it to agents and publishers as the first book about philanthropy written from a donor's perspective, a book that would help save the future of giving. But I was told that a book about philanthropy just wasn't so interesting. Until, remarkably, my work in social justice (that big philanthropic driver) provided the turning point.

In early 2019, Joel Braunold, whose name you may recognize from Chapter Five, held an event at our house. Joel was stepping down as Executive Director of the Alliance for Middle East Peace (ALLMEP), and part of the event's purpose was to introduce his successor, a lifelong peace activist named John Lyndon. Anyway, we all had dinner and got to talking about the book. I asked Joel at one point if he could recommend a good agent, and he kindly said he'd think about it. Apparently, Joel wasn't kidding, as I got a text from him shortly thereafter. He and John were sitting on a plane bound for San Francisco, and they were chatting, and John mentioned a dinner he'd be attending later in the month (a dinner whose purpose was also the promotion of ALLMEP) with J. K. Rowling's agent. 'Would it be okay,' Joel asked, 'if John told him about your book?'

You can imagine my response. A few days later, Neil Blair of The Blair Partnership emailed that he'd love to connect, and he'd have his assistant set up a call. All good, until Natasha, Neil's assistant, followed up with a date and time. Well, it turned out that I'd be in Tel Aviv (for a board meeting) when Natasha was proposing I speak with Neil, and the UK/Israel time difference meant that the call would occur in the wee hours of the morning. If I were twenty, I don't think I'd have had the guts to say, 'I'll actually be in Tel Aviv then. Could we find another time?' (After all, this was J. K. Rowling's agent.) But I went ahead and said it – and discovered, in the process, that Neil would be in Tel Aviv too. So, we went for a lovely coffee at one of my favorite Tel Aviv hotels, only to realize that we'd both been working for film studios at the same time, way back when. Neil was keenly aware of the issues facing philanthropy and, soon after our meeting, he introduced me to the head of his literary division, Rory Scarfe – who has been an absolutely fantastic advocate for this book. The rest, as they say, is history.

So, thank you to Joel, John, Neil, and Rory. This wouldn't have happened without you.

To my HarperCollins team: Lydia, Harriet, Anna, Sim, and the rest, thank you for believing in this project. Your professionalism and care are so appreciated.

Thanks, too, to my initial co-writer, Julie Gruenbaum Fax, who helped in the early days of the book and, as a journalist, conducted many of the initial interviews. And to the many wonderful friends and colleagues who agreed to speak with us about your thoughts on and experiences with philanthropy: I owe you a debt of gratitude. Many of your stories and so much of your wisdom have been included in the book, or else gave me perspective and guidance throughout its writing. I'm so very grateful for your time and encouragement. Special thanks for their amazing support go to Daniel Sokatch, David Myers, Jen Spitzer (my partner in creating our wonderful, progressive DAF program), JT (my amazing social media associate), Melody Young, Jay Stein, Rachel Fine, Raphe Sonenshein, and Imam Abdullah Antepli. I'm grateful as well to rabbis Sarah Bassin, Rachel Sabath Beit-Halachmi, Jill Jacobs, and Mary Zamore for the expert guidance and perspective. And to Baila, thanks for always believing.

Jules: without your encouragement and finagling to get Larissa to agree to write this with me, there would be no book. And Larissa, it was absolutely *beshert* that we would work together, and I couldn't wish for a better co-conspirator. We did it!

Finally, thank you to my husband, best friend and partner, Josh, and to my family. I'm so blessed and grateful for you all.

'Lisa Greer's guidebook invites us to accompany her through her personal and pioneering journey into transforming the world of philanthropy by making a difference. This "how to" book is not to be missed on our path ahead confronting threatening global challenges that come home to roost.

Lisa's writing reminds us that through giving we transform ourselves through work tied to the etymological meaning of the word "philanthropy"—love of humanity. She warns us that this can only happen by recognizing that our intertwined lives and careers can advance only through transactional trust aligning our interests and actions focused on outcomes.

Greer's presentation and interpretation about giving, insights about its future, and the role of nonprofit, for-profit, profit-for-purpose businesses, innovations, startups, individuals and technology in rebuilding our world are required reading. This book is important for every global citizen joining her call for an impact revolution to build meaningful lives. She calls for a renewed focus to build lasting change based on outcomes that blend wealth management with philanthropy and new pathways integrated into interdependent lives and lifestyles.

In Hebrew, the biblical commandment of giving (ונתנו) is a palindrome— it reads backward as it does forward. Ancient texts taught us that to give is not to be diminished but rather to be enabled once again to give in equal measure. Moving beyond charity as an emotional response to rescue and relief, her book calls for a return to philanthropy aligned with its original meaning— contributing to long-term strategies that rebuild our world. The book links "feeling good" ineluctably to "doing good" by strategies and tactics that blend teams, organizations, and investments leading towards change that increases the welfare of others.'

Glenn Yago, Senior Director of Milken Innovation Center at the Jerusalem Institute, Hebrew University of Jerusalem School of Business